National Socialism
Its Principles and Philosophy

Carlos Videla

National Socialism
Its Principles and Philosophy

Carlos Videla

Copyright © 2020 Sanctuary Press Ltd

All rights reserved. No part of this book may be reproduced in any form by any electronic or mechanical means including photocopying, recording, or information storage and retrieval without permission in writing from the publisher.

ISBN-13: 978-1-912887-64-4

Sanctuary Press Ltd
71-75 Shelton Street
Covent Garden
London
WC2H 9JQ

www.sanctuarypress.com
Email: info@sanctuarypress.com

Contents

Introduction	5
The Law of Life	9
Biological Worldview	18
The Worldview And Politics	21
The Worldview Origin	25
Developers of the NS-Worldview	27
Sources of the NS-Worldview	29
NS-Worldview and Ideological Instruction	31
NS-Worldview and Science	34
NS-Worldview Symbols	37
Enemies of the NS-Worldview	39
The Law of Struggle	43
The Father of All Things	47
Nietzschean Legacy	50
Nietzsche Prophet of the NS-Worldview	56
Heraclitus' Vision of the World	59
Strife as Cultural Foundation	65
Warrior Ethics	69
Struggle as Divine Order	72
The Way of Heroic Realism	76
The Law of Selection	81
The Biological Sense of Selection	83
Selection and Human Groups	87
The Nordic Race	90
Nordic Transnational	94
Counter-Selection	96
The Convoy of Death	101
Fountain of Life	103

The Führer Principle	105
The Order of the Clans	108
Fertility Law	111
Fertility and Politics	112
Fertility and Inventive Genius	118
Artist and Soldier	123
Fertility and Economy	125
Economic Biology	132
Monumentality	134
The Danger of Monumentality	136
Heredity Law	143
Heredity Science	145
Mate Selection	149
Evolutionist Synthesis	151
Racial Biology	154
The Ancestor's Heritage	157
The Body's Great Reason	160
New Rational Science	163
Special Path	169
Twilight of the Idols	177
Spiritual Chaos	181
Eidetic Imagery	184
Spirit or Blood	186
Crusade Against Mysticism	190
Aktion Hess	193
Twilight of Men	199
The Defeat of the Worldview	207
Bibliography	213

Introduction

Without a doubt National Socialism is one of the most disconcerting phenomena of modern times. Nearly a hundred years since its foundation, the Nazi movement still excites an undeniable interest, and in some cases, obsession. Hitler's book *Mein Kampf* is widely sold in many countries. In the United States an e-book version reached the top of the Amazon bestseller list in 2014. The book has been available again in Germany only since December 31, 2015, when the state of Bavaria lost the copyright that had kept it virtually suppressed. "Germany trembles at the return of *Mein Kampf*", proclaimed the headlines, an accurate reflection of the establishment's feelings towards a renewed interest in National Socialism: an ideology mythologized by the same powers who have attempted to hang a veil over it.

Interest in National Socialism is a universal phenomenon. It goes far beyond the confines of so-called "neo-Nazism", and reveals an unsettling and widespread attraction.

However, since the postwar period a truthful and transparent approach to this ideology has always remained elusive. Researchers seem to drift when interpreting the Nazi phenomenon and, due to an inability to delve into the foundations of this ideology, their investigations devolve into uninteresting simplifications and unconvincing conclusions. The most common approach is to pass off National Socialism as a movement without ideological substance, which merely reacted to events, took advantage of political upheavals and, in some mysterious way, hypnotized the masses with the hysterical rhapsody of anti-Semitism. Thus National Socialism has been stereotyped as a creed as baseless as it was incoherent.

But National Socialism did, in fact, have a profound and cogent ideology, or better said, a worldview (weltanschauung). A Worldview based on certain laws, which were the pillars of the various Nazi theories and policies. Without an understanding of this Worldview, all political and historical analysis of Nazism must remain incomplete.

Even though the National Socialist Worldview was born under the auspices of a political movement, these can be studied and compared, revealing the rather apolitical and even universal character of the former. In this sense, the Nazi Worldview can set aside the jackboots, the uniforms and the parades and still preserve its essence.

This book seeks to shed light on this elusive foundation, through analysis of official texts used in the ideological instruction of National Socialists. These primary sources have been largely neglected by scholars of Nazism, partly because of their disappearance as a result of postwar censorship, but also because many researchers were carried away by the vague and conformist ideas that characterized the first stage of National Socialism studies. The works of Nazi intellectuals have also been considered, because although written in personal rather than public capacity, they fall within and serve to illuminate the ideological limits of the Worldview. The opinions of those researchers who have managed to overcome the barriers of academic standardization are also included, along with certain aphorisms of Nietzsche, considered by Nazism as prophetic foreshadowings of what would become the National Socialist Worldview.

Nowadays, the task of bringing to light the ideological foundation of Nazism is relatively easy. The sources are available again through digital media and the internet. The texts are neither obscure nor impenetrable, but rather the opposite, they are clear and simple, and attempt to convey the Worldview to a mass audience. The truly difficult task is recognizing that so much of what we think we know about Nazism is erroneous, or at least biased, and that therefore researchers and their audiences, both for and against Nazism, have allowed themselves to be carried away by a rather abstract and vague idea of the movement.

The mature historical perspective that emerges with the passage of time ought now to allow for Nazism to be investigated like any

Introduction

other historical occurrence. Seventy years of simplifications must be left behind in order to understand the bewildering phenomenon of National Socialism.

Overcoming that barrier is not easy. It is an invitation to those adventurous and nonconformist spirits who dare to examine pages censured by official historiography. Uncovering the ideological foundations of Nazism, with a free spirit and an open mind, can be a true intellectual adventure.

The Law of Life

Dieter Schwarz, the pseudonym of SS Major (*SS-Brigadeführer*) Franz Albert Six, discovered in the 1930s that the the enemies of Nazism. were engaged in a deliberate strategy abroad to obscure National Socialist ideology. Their goal was to make the National Socialist Worldview a mysterious, confusing and remote ideology.

> Any attack on the National Socialist Worldview is an attack on the National Socialist State, since this State rests on that Worldview. These attacks which come especially from the German émigrés, accuse us of materialism, anti-christianity or Caesarism. Other emigrants have claimed we have embarked on a crusade of racist bestiality, or collectivist absolutism. Others argue that National Socialism is linked to theosophy. Thus, they continue ad absurdum[1].

Their efforts to make the Nazi ideology inaccessible managed to create a diffuse image abroad, an image that prevailed in the world even after the defeat of the *Third Reich*, a phenomenon that has lasted even up to the present.

In the postwar period it has been repeatedly claimed that the foundation of Nazism was anti-Semitism. That Nazism was simply a hatred of Jews and its sole political objective was their destruction. An ideology conceived to hate and destroy. But analyzing this thesis historically is problematic. The retired US Army Colonel, R. H. S. Stolfi, in his biography of Hitler, raises significant doubts of the importance of anti-Semitism as the ideological axis of Nazism. Stolfi states that even though no one can deny that National Socialism pointed to Jews as the enemies responsible for many of the sorrows that afflicted German society, the

---

1   Dieter Schwarz. *Attack Against the National Socialist Worldview*

intangibility of these enemies for the people meant they were practically removed from Nazi discourse from the year 1923 onwards.

> "[Hitler] maintained personal detachment from the German Jews and cannot be seen to have hated them in the sense of gutter, religious, anti-Semitism."

> "Hitler would pursue tough courses of political action throughout the 1920s that would involve little and often no anti-Semitism after a noisy beginning in 1920... And in 1923, the year of the near-destruction of Germany, Hitler would see the enemy as Marxists, November Criminals, provincial Separatists, and the French—but hardly German Jews."

> "We see relatively little anti-Semitism in the face of these issues and the reorganization of the party from 1925 through 1928... In the early 1930s we see the same dearth of anti-Semitism on Hitler's part as compared with his greater concentration on other issues."

> "The [economic] situation would intensify in 1931 and double in numbers of unemployed by 1932, the year of the five great elections. In such a situation, anti-Semitic propaganda could not have had much effect on Hitler's goal of seizing power....anti-Semitism could not have been either an effective propaganda theme or high priority for Hitler from 1930 through 1935."

Norman H. Baynes, in his two-volume, 1,980-page collection of Hitler's speeches, could annotate: "It is surprising to observe how little the Fuehrer has said on the treatment of the Jews by the National Socialist State." And Speer could comment that it had repeatedly surprised him, in later years, that "scarcely any anti-Semitic remarks of Hitler have remained in my memory." ...in his collected wartime monologues Hitler may have spent more time discussing the Jews, but still only a miniscule amount compared with other subjects.[2]

---

2   R. H. S. Stolfi. *Hitler, Beyond Evil and Tyranny*

Lothrop Stoddart, a renowned American intellectual and contemporary of National Socialism, recounts something similar in his chronicle of travels across the *Reich*. Stoddart records the lack of interest in the "Jewish question" by civilians and politicians. And surprisingly, this lack of interest is again confirmed by the hundreds of the *Führer's* speeches published in the postwar period by Max Domarus, where the Jews are mentioned hundreds of times in the editor's commentary, but very few times in the speeches themselves. The lack of anti-Semitism in official speeches and publications is disconcerting and at the very least allows us to question its true importance as an ideological foundation of National Socialism.

However, it is impossible to ignore the fact that the so-called "Jewish problem" was an important issue for National Socialism in certain periods, especially during the war. At that time, anti-Semitic rhetoric was reignited in response to the alleged responsibility of prominent members of the international Jewish community, for the outbreak of the world war.

Given this ambivalent attitude, and alternating interest and disinterest in Judaism, the first question arises regarding the foundation of Nazism. How did an ideology, which has been accused of building itself purely on hatred against Jews, go such long periods without mentioning the reason for its very existence?

Another aspect of Nazism emphasized by scholars was its anti-Marxism. Marxism was certainly an enemy of Nazism, there is no doubt about that, but so too was political Christianity, liberalism and conservatism. But the Marxist threat was completely neutralized during the first months of government. Just as the political right and the conservative reactionaries, were promptly expelled from the government and then removed from the political scene. Political Christianity, and Freemasonry were also driven out of public life. So the question that arises, if these enemies were removed from the public and political scene, how could Nazism have justified its existence for the forthcoming years on behalf of a *Reich* that claimed to be millennial? The answer to this question was that Nazism had an ideological foundation that did not depended on the existence of its opponents, an ideology that achieved its own expression within the party, and one that would have undoubtedly sustained the *Reich* for a thousand years - irrespective of the question of the 'Jews', — who at best were no more than a minor irritant to the *Reich* — or the 'Marxists', or 'Freemasonry', or any other opposing ideology. Even if the enemies of National Socialism had been others or if they had not existed at all, this Movement had a purpose based on its own worldview. Its ideological essence was permanent, and one that had completely different objectives from all other ideologies.

As we have now addressed the "anti" as a foundation of National Socialism, we can now considered the other key ideas that it is claimed formed the basis of Nazi ideology. The purity of the Aryan race would seem to be the next candidate. In that sense National Socialism could have been conceived as the effort to preserve this race, saving it from mixing, in order to create a society of Nordic clones free of problems or social injustices. But the issue of racial mixing was almost nonexistent at that time in the *Reich*, and the idea of a homogeneous community as the foundation of some utopian society was something that no one in National Socialism postulated. Hitler on the contrary laughed at the *Volkisch* ideology, or racial nationalism, noting how the Germans, at the times when they allowed themselves to be drowned in beer at the taverns, transformed the spirit of brotherhood and Volkisch ideology into instinctive aggressiveness and violence.

For Hitler, racial purity and national homogeneity in itself did not mean so much as it was later claimed in the postwar period. A quick review of the texts of the Nazi racial theory denotes that the German people were a repository of several racial heritages, evidencing therefore that there was no indication that the Nazis wanted to marginalize part of their own population. The idea of producing a new social division, this time between Nordic and non-Nordic, was definitely rejected by Hitler and National Socialism. Furthermore, Hitler was not particularly involved in racial hygiene issues or anthropological problems. In his *Table Talk* (Tischgespräche im Führerhauptquartier), also known as, *Conversations at the Headquarters* or *The Bormann Notes*, a postwar document that includes the transcripts with Hitler's intimate circle of lieutenants, there were few references to the Aryans, and almost nothing about the superiority of the Nordic race.

In the collection of speeches of Max Domarus, a text of more than 3,300 pages, the word Aryan or references to the Nordic race, in more than 13 years of compilation, scarcely appears as mentioned by Hitler. As it is, there were no great speeches by Hitler on intricate anthropological theories. Homogeneity or racial purity simply was not the ultimate goal of Nazism, however much racial dynamics featured in Nazi analysis as a determining factor of history. As indicated in the ideological text *Why Do We Fight?*

> Our racial ideas are just an expression of our worldview.

On the other hand, National Socialism has been defined as nationalism, the most revolutionary and socialist, but nationalism none the less. A movement that based its struggle and objectives on the defence of a particular nation, Germany. Nevertheless, this seems again a hypothesis with significant nuances to be crowned as the great foundation of Nazism. In his book *Mein Kampf*, Hitler explained how during his years in Vienna, as a worker he realized that the primary necessity of every worker was first to get his daily bread - the worker did not worry about abstractions such as nation or identity. Hitler rejected the idea of asking an almost starving people to develop a patriotic nationalist attitude.

The SS led the process of creating a new concept of the State that could surpass the narrow margin of the Sovereign National State, a political idea that had actually fragmented European unity.

> It was not until the nineteenth century that the idea of nationalism was carried out to an eccentric extreme, exacerbating to an unhealthy degree the natural difference between peoples who experienced, until the bloody European civil wars, the last remnant of continental consciousness.[3]

---

3   *Teaching Plan for Worldview Education of the SS and Police.* SS-Hauptamt

National Socialism - Its Principles and Philosophy

This Nazi policy deepened the history of disagreements between National Socialism and German nationalists. And although National Socialism entered the government in an alliance with the German Nationalist People's Party (DNVP), within six months it rid itself of this uncomfortable ally, in a seldom studied violent purge. This alliance, just like the Nazi-Soviet one or the alliances made with the German Communist Party during the strikes of 1932, could not be sustained.

The National Socialist attack on German nationalism was overwhelming and used intimidation and force. The so-called second revolution from March to July 1933, this time against the reactionaries (die Reaktion), removed from all political positions the nationalists and conservatives that were pursuing their own agenda. Hermann Beck, a researcher on the relationship between the National Socialist Party and the DNVP, reports on this situation.

> "The tendency to disregard Nazi attacks on German Nationalists and their supporters in the conservative Bürgertum [bourgeoisie] is connected with a failure—or possibly an unwillingness—to recognize the social revolutionary overtones of the Nazi movement, in particular the Nazis' loathing of the "Bürgertum, its values, and its entire bourgeois way of life, which many Nazis saw reflected in the DNVP. "

Two main reasons may explain the tendency to disregard the open conflict between the Nazis and their conservative alliance partner. First, the overt cooperation between Mussolini and conservative elites in Italy…Secondly, the Marxist interpretation of fascism, emphasized the connection between fascism and the capitalist bourgeoisie.

> The numerous incidences of unbridled violence directed against conservative *Honoratioren* [dignitaries] and DNVP members show that the *Bündnis der Eliten* (pact of elites) was suspended during the *Machtergreifung* [takeover], as many local Nazi and SA leaders violently turned against local conservative elites.

The Law of Life

> By this point, Nazism had succeeded in putting itself forward as a protest movement against bourgeois lifestyles... The Nazis' scorn and contempt for German conservatism and the classes that supported it...burst forth violently during the *Machtergreifung*. Conservatives were considered unfit to have any share in the governance of Germany, blamed for the halfhearted conduct of the war, and accused of cowardice in 1918. There was a broad consensus among Nazis about not wanting to hear themselves mentioned in the same breath as conservatives.[4]

Regarding the foundation of Nazism, the theory of National Socialism has been also framed within the phenomenon of so-called European "fascisms."

Leon Degrelle, leader of the Belgian Rexists, a movement with Christian and monarchical roots included in the group of "generic fascism", rejected this thesis, distancing National Socialism from this phenomenon.

> Italian fascism was very different from German National Socialism. Socially, the German position was bolder. Fascism was more Christian and more conservative. Hitler had liquidated the last vestiges of the Empire, whereas Mussolini, although reluctantly, continued being the duster of the King. If the movements in Germany and Italy were different, what of the other European fascist movements? Romanian fascism was almost mystical. Their leader Codreanu arrived mounted on horseback and dressed in white to political demonstrations. They called him the Archangel. Portuguese fascism was dispassionate; Professor Salazar fixed the points of his doctrine in an intellectually cold manner. Also Norway was something else. Quisling was as cheerful as a gravedigger. He relied on militias whose boots were much brighter than his doctrine. England had the fascism of the aristocrat Mosley. Among the many French fascist parties the feature that they all had

---

4   Hermann Beck. *The Fateful Alliance, German Conservatives and Nazi in 1933*

in common was confusion. In Spain, Jose Antonio, despite his inheritance as Señorito, was an inspired speaker, but this splendid young man saw his dream shattered by a firing squad.[5]

Although Degrelle himself spoke about a spiritual communion of these movements, he failed to find a concrete ideological concept that each had in common. Degrelle observed that what has been called "generic fascism" was in fact a political conglomerate with many ideological differences, different origins, foundations, and very different political realities. Some fell into the realm of revolutionary movements but, others were definitely part of the conservative reaction. That is why, independently of the political pacts reached, Hitler felt affinity towards certain specific leaders rather than with specific movements and parties. Among the leaders whom Hitler admired was Mussolini, but not his fascist doctrine. Also, Hitler admired Leon Degrelle, praising his courage when commanding the *Wallonian* Waffen SS legion of volunteers, but not the doctrines of his Catholic and monarchical party. Another leader admired by Hitler was the Romanian general Ian Antonescu, whose *Legion of the Archangel Michael* — a movement that was classified as *fascist*, and known as the *Iron Guard*, but was later crushed with the approval of the *Führer*. With other leaders of this "generic fascism", Hitler maintained merely circumstantial alliances. He never valued Franco and was less enthusiastic about Franco's improvised and reactionary political syncretism called the "Traditionalist Spanish Phalanx of the Committees of the National Syndicalist Offensive" Finally, moving away from the so-called fascist ideology, Hitler even came to admire Stalin.

Neither can we seek the foundation of Nazism in the totalitarian idea or in the dictatorial political system. Although National Socialism acquired such a structure, it was not thought to be essential for its future functioning.

In a conversation recorded in April 1942 and published in the postwar period in *Table Talk*, Hitler established the foundations of a republican

---

5   Leon Degrelle. *Hitler for a Thousand Years*

National Socialist State, where the Head of State should be elected by a popular representative body with attributions tending to balance the executive power of the State's *Führer*. Hitler also established in this conversation a rigorous separation of the legislative and executive power. This plan was confirmed by Joseph Goebbels, minister of Public Instruction and Propaganda, who gave details in his personal diary dated September 1943, about the future republican configuration of a Senatorial College designed for the election of future leaders of the State. Perhaps for this reason Hitler never re-created the State nor changed the republican Constitution of Weimar times, but ruled indefinitely under State decrees of emergency. Therefore, National Socialism did not define its governmental political structure before its destruction, but everything indicates that it was regarded as a momentary product of historical emergency.

The final idea which remains to be examined is Nazism as a socialist-nationalist system comprised of left-wing ideas synthesized with nationalist ideology. The problem here is to define that system precisely. No detailed sociopolitical theory can be salvaged from this definition. Neither does National Socialism have a definite economic theory, but as the official texts indicate, economic theory was subordinated to essential objectives.

National Socialism may well have been racist, nationalist, identitarian, socialist, anti-Jewish, anti-Marxist, anti-capitalist, and on and on. It also had a 25-point programme and tried to reestablish national pride, regain territories, annul the Treaty of Versailles, and depart from capitalism. But all of this was not its basic ideology but rather its derivative, and as such, could be excluded from the political scene without affecting the essence of National Socialism.

Applying merely political or economic criteria, Nazism can have a thousand faces, all depending on the prism through which you look. True understanding of the elusive ideological foundation of National Socialism can only begin to emerge by focusing on the National Socialist Worldview.

BIOLOGICAL WORLDVIEW

The National Socialist Worldview was not a mysterious ideology, neither was it connected to impenetrable philosophical ideas, nor was it the fruit of political or economic theoretical abstractions. The National Socialist Worldview sought to increase the value of heritable biological characteristics in order to achieve evolutionary improvement sustained over time at a community level. This was understood as a divine mandate based on the fulfillment of eternal and inescapable laws of nature. These were called *"Life Laws"* (*Lebensgesetz*) and on them Nazism built its Worldview.

To fulfill these laws Nazism tried to rid itself of all kinds of abstractions by focusing on those rules that govern both the simplest organisms on earth and the most complex, human beings. This would lead to an increase in development, progress and general welfare. With this Worldview, National Socialism set itself the task of establishing a new political and cultural order.

The principle *Life Law* for the National Socialist Worldview was the *Law of Struggle* (*Kampfgesetz*), the motivating principle of the whole existence and essence of all beings. Beneath this law were the *Law of Selection* (*Gesetz der Auslese*), the *Law of Fertility* (*Gesetz der Fruchtbarkeit*), and the *Law of Inheritance* (*Gesetz des Vererbung*); laws that would allow the physiological development required for the increase of value in nature.

The Nazi Worldview understood existence as one tremendous struggle. In this Worldview the universe was in constant flux, which forced beings to adapt to ever-changing environmental conditions. This *Law of Struggle* produced constant selection as observed by the NS-Worldview in nature, where not everyone managed to transfer their heritable traits, which meant that no generation was equal to the previous one. The key to Nazi thinking was to understand that selection was what created organisms, species and races and not the other way around. Race was understood as a derivative of selection, as were evolutionary improvement and development. For Nazism, the selective processes were more important than the race itself.

The Law of Life

The *Law of Fertility*, meanwhile, was a prerequisite for the development of the *Law of Selection*. For the Nazi Worldview, as more heritable characteristics came into play with the environment and were subjected to selection, the greater the value of those attributes which survived the struggle for existence. Therefore, according to National Socialism, no one ought to exclude themselves from having as many children as possible, since from all this trial and error came the selection of effective heritable traits in the struggle for preservation.

The transfer of heritable traits was carried out under the aegis of the *Law of Inheritance*, a dynamic that would transmit the hereditary characteristics necessary to overcome the struggle for existence. Knowing the *Law of Inheritance* allowed the biological configuration of offspring to be anticipated, thereby orienting procreation to toward objectives of evolutionary improvement.

National Socialism was completely devoted to the furtherance of these laws. That was its motivation for political and cultural struggle. The main manuals of instruction in the NS-Worldview, those texts only for leaders (*Nur für Führer*), especially those edited by the "SS Main Office" (*SS-Hauptamt*), were explicit in this objective.

> National Socialism has declared that it has as its goal the restoration of natural vital order and will use the necessary force to restore the natural laws of man.[6]

For National Socialism, these *Life Laws* were the basis of all biological development and the only mechanism that nature has to increase an organism's capacity for struggle and evolutionary value.

> The National Socialist revolution is the advancement of life itself, its objective is the free development of the natural forces of our people, its meaning is in the fulfillment of the eternal, the divine *Life-Laws* of nature.[7].

---

6   SS-Hauptamt. *SS-Man and Blood Questions.*
7   SS-Hauptamt . *Racial Policy*

On these laws the National Socialist Worldview built its entire ethics and ideology, and all of its political and philosophical concepts. The official dictionary of Nazi ideology, edited by the SS (*NS-Wörterbuch*), pointed to these laws as the fundamental part of the ideological lexicon.

> Events in nature are subject to immutable laws. The human mind has been able to get an idea of many natural laws. Within the laws of nature, the *Life-Laws* stand out in a special place. Man must respect and follow them. Peoples and races that believe that they are capable of ignoring them fall into degeneracy and decay. Examples of Life Laws: the *Law of Struggle*, the *Law of Fertility*, the *Law of Selection*, etc.[8]

The basic existential dynamics of beings also derived from these laws. Among them we find the struggle for "living space" (*Lebensraum*), "environmental influence" (*Unwelteinflüsse*), "breeding laws" (*Zuchtgesetz*), "proper mate selection" (*Gattenwahl*), as well as the "Leader principle" (*Führerprinzip*) and "racial characteristics" (*Rassenmerkmale*).

For National Socialism, because these natural laws had been forgotten and replaced by abstract ideologies and fantasies that rejected human nature, it had led to the great crisis of the West. If National Socialism were to continue down that same path, the human race would be doomed.

> The laws of nature are valid for all forms of life. It is therefore necessary to know these laws and, their observance is the prerequisite of their preservation and the subsequent evolution of life. Failure to observe these laws means decay, deformity, and ultimately ruin. National Socialism has made the restoration of this natural order of life an objective and has endowed the application of the laws of nature to man with the will of the State.[9]

---

8   SS-Hauptamt. *NS Dictionary*
9   SS-Hauptamt. *Believe and Fight*

The Law of Life

For the Nazi ideology, continuing to dissociate and deviate from natural laws would enhance characteristics that had nothing to do with nature's processes of selection, and lead humanity to extinction.

> This planet will once again follow its orbit through the ether, devoid of human life,[10]

Western ideologies were, for the National Socialist Worldview, ideologies of extinction and death, ideologies that denied the natural inheritance of men.

The laws of the National Socialist Worldview challenged the entire Western cultural tradition, a tradition that understands man as a combination of a natural and a supernatural essence, giving to what has been called soul, mind, spirit, etc. an essence that would seek to escape the *Laws of Life*. The laws of the NS-Worldview opposed this dualistic tradition of the West, both in its religious and rationalistic varieties. As a result of this, National Socialism confronted all kinds of doctrines, religions, philosophies and mysticisms that attributed to man an essence or origin other than the natural.

But this return to nature did not involve a simple movement toward environmentalism, or flora and fauna. Nor did it have anything to do with experiences that sought a mystical union with the goddess of nature, or a "natural life" obsessed with "natural products", the outdoors, or muscle mass. The laws of the NS-Worldview had no relation with the ethical theory known as "*Jusnatura*" or to theories about "natural rights." For National Socialism a real approach to nature meant recognizing the relentless *Laws of Life* as laws which affect men just as they affect all other organisms on earth.

THE WORLDVIEW AND POLITICS

The first step toward a proper understanding of the Nazi Worldview is to separate it from political ideology. Worldview and politics, although

---

10   Adolf Hitler, *Mein Kampf*.

related, had different characteristics.

> Political parties are prone to make compromises, but a Worldview never does this. A political party even reckons with opponents, but a Worldview proclaims its own infallibility.[11]

For Goebbels, the NS-Worldview gave meaning to political struggle.

> National Socialism is really a Worldview. It always begins at the beginning and lays new foundations for life. That is why our task is so difficult, but also so beautiful.[12]

Hitler claimed that National Socialism was not for export, that is, it was a movement limited to Germany. In spite of this, Hitler made efforts to adapt the fundamental aspects of the NS-Worldview for the various governments which were allied to the *Reich*. This apparent contradiction begins to dissipate when the National Socialist Worldview is separated from the National Socialist German Workers Party or NSDAP (*Nationalsozialistische Deutsche Arbeiterpartei*). The Nazi Party was one of the many vectors of the Worldview, a tool confined to Germany's political problems and historical moment. Its founders created an organization based on those conditions and that cultural heritage formed a unique and inimitable political structure.

The political objectives of National Socialism were derivative of the NS-Worldview. "Intellectual" Nazi theories on social and economic policies are difficult to come by, as are learned Nazi treatises on economics or sociology. National Socialism had millennial goals, therefore it could not base its ideology on some economic or social theory that would soon expire. Hitler did not base his Worldview on economic, sociological, or philosophical textbooks, but on the Book of Life of Earth's organisms. But this was not clear to all National Socialists. Ernst Röhm, the leader of the "Assault Division" (SA) and the Strasser brothers, among others, paid with their lives for their

---

11   Hitler. *Mein Kampf*
12   Joseph Goebbels. *The Goebbels Diaries 1942 - 1943*

The Law of Life

insistence on keeping the Nazi revolution within the limits of the political spectrum, never understanding the radical objectives of the NS-Worldview.

> Anyone who believes that the völkisch National Socialist State should distinguish itself from the other States only mechanically, as it were, through the better construction of its economic life— thanks to a better equilibrium between poverty and riches, or to a fairer wage-system, or to the elimination of vast differences in the scale of salaries— understands only the superficial features of our Movement and has not the least idea of what we mean when we speak of our Worldview.
>
> All these features just mentioned could not guarantee us a lasting existence and certainly would be no warranty of greatness. A nation that could content itself with external reforms, would not have the slightest chance of success in the general struggle for life among the nations of the world. A movement that confined its missions to such adjustments, however right and equitable, would effect no far-reaching or profound reform of the existing order. The whole effect of such measures would be limited to externals. They would not furnish the nation with the moral armament which alone will enable it to effectively overcome the weaknesses from which we are suffering today.[13]

Time and again researchers are left perplexed when they try to systematize the policies of Nazism by means of theoretical systems or schools of thought. It's not that economics and politics did not follow any norm, the problem is that the logic that underpinned them has been overlooked.

> Our worldview is the foundation of life. For National Socialism this Worldview is not a philosophical concept. It is rather the fundamental question that controls existence. Our Worldview is not a theory, because then the struggle for power would not

---

13   Hitler. *Mein Kampf*

make sense. The Worldview is the foundation of the centuries to come. The Movement has no catechism for behavior in daily life. National Socialist teaching must lead to a natural foundation of life. Our Worldview must be rooted in the people as a vital element.[14]

The socialism of National Socialism must be seen from this perspective. While many leaders of social justice sought ideological foundations in sociological or economic theories, Nazi socialism was filled with vitalist analogies, sinking its roots into the natural aspect of the collective unity, the foundation that sustains the species. Currently scholars are looking for the links between Nazi socialism and the doctrine of political socialism, but Nazi socialism had no essential relation to international socialism, it was based on gregarious instincts embedded in genetic inheritance, those instincts that made members of a species act together for self-preservation. According to Nazi socialism, the bourgeois, nobility and reactionaries, with their elitist policies based on money and privileges, elevated counter-selective processes which undermined the *Laws of Life*. Therein lies the reason for National Socialism's anti-bourgeois or anti-capitalist policies. Nazi socialism was not essentially a quest for social justice or the restoration of rights to establish a more equitable society, the latter was an outcome of the Worldview. For Hitler, nature did not seek equity, but an increase in value and preservation.

The same is true of Nazi nationalism. It was not based on the nineteenth-century abstraction of the nation-state. On the contrary, National Socialism tried to dilute the bases of the rule of law eagerly defended by German nationalists. Nazi nationalism was the expression of the struggle for the existence of a specific human group. Nazi nationalism was not a nationalist chauvinism or the defense of a flag, of an imaginary group constructed out of historical convenience. The nation defended by the Nazis was the nation of a human group with a common genetic background, a human conglomerate created through

---

14 Heinz Oskar Schaefer. *General Aspects of the National Socialist Worldview* in *Educational Writings for National Politics*. Vol. I

millennia of struggle against the environment by a selective process. A human group that had no borders and that was governed only by natural law. Nazi nationalism, therefore, confronted Marxists and liberals whose policies sought to dilute the natural frontiers derived from selection. It also confronted, for the same reasons, nationalists and bourgeois who were anchored in an abstract vision of the nation.

National Socialism was therefore a socialism and a nationalism at the same time, and had its roots in the deepest atavism of human nature and did not conform to any revolutionary socialism or bourgeois nationalism. National Socialism was neither corporatist nor capitalist nor socialist. Neither liberal, conservative, reactionary, or socialist. It took what was necessary from all kinds of ideologies, using all the tools that it found to promote policies that encouraged the selection and preservation of a specific group with heritable characteristics.

THE WORLDVIEW ORIGIN

With the exception of Hitler's works, much of the well-known Nazi literature that has come down to us and which might serve as a source for studying National Socialist ideology is not actually the most essential for the purpose. Some texts were written prior to the formation of the Party, others were published in its first stage, when the Worldview was not yet fully developed, and others are privately published books without official recognition from the Party and often to the distaste of Hitler. And while sources from the official stage of ideological consolidation are slowly emerging that seemed to be lost after the collapse of National Socialism, many were irrevocably destroyed. Researchers therefore make methodological errors in using unofficial books as ideological material of the first order, or by mixing ideology produced in a precarious initial stage with distilled material produced by official organs.

The National Socialist Worldview had its birth in Hitler's book *Mein Kampf*. Initially, only the *Führer* was clear about the fundamentals of this Worldview. In his book, especially in the chapter "People and Race" (*Volk und Rasse*), Hitler established the ideological bases that would be elaborated upon during the years of the *Third Reich*. Also important is his posthumously published work called "the Second Book" (*Zweites Buch*), especially its opening chapters. Private speeches and talks, published in various formats and under various titles during the postwar period, fill in the pieces of the Hitlerist Worldview.

During the years of political struggle, the Worldview was present in a latent and somewhat veiled way. Only with the creation of the SS at Hitler's request did this Worldview begin to take a more systematic form. With the years, and when the official entities were established, the NS-Worldview acquired an elaborate form. This process was not exempt from trial and error. Some authors contradict each other, since the different organs of the Movement contributed particular points of view. On the other hand, within the Movement there were different factions that only remained united by Hitler's authority. Given the lack of initial collaboration and due to the political struggle, these groups competed for control of the ideological doctrine. Neo-pagan mystics, socialist revolutionaries and nationalists, among others, struggled to influence Nazism with their ideas. Even hierarchs like Rosenberg or Himmler needed several ideological corrections by Hitler to allay their utopian ideas. Hitler reproached Rosenberg for the theories in his book *The Myth of the Twentieth Century* and never allowed it to be included in the official bibliography of the Party. Himmler was also criticized in the *Table Talks* when it came to racial utopias. The SS plan for the *Germanization* of Europe was looked down on by Hitler, who, doubted that the term meant anything concrete.

The NS-Worldview followed a process of elaboration under Hitler's strict supervision. Once in power and in control of the state, Hitler put the Movement in order, allowing for the consolidation of its ideology along his own lines, a difficult task given the initial syncretism. This work was carried out mainly by a new generation of Nazis and within the institutional frameworks of official organizations for ideological production. They were mainly SS intellectuals, young people who had finished their university degrees just before the war. These officers had been educated in a culture where the old liberal values and ideologies had no influence, and for that reason they did not experience the ideological confusion which many Nazis of the first generation had felt.

Developers of the NS-Worldview

The developers of the NS-Worldview were a group of intellectuals and scientists in charge of ideological instruction attached to the Movement and especially the SS. Although the Worldview took its first official steps in *Mein Kampf*, hundreds of intellectuals expanded upon its guidelines. Their areas of interest were varied, and personal accents gave rise to important nuances, but it is at the intersection from which all these official works emanated, and to which they converged, that the National Socialist Worldview can be observed.

Christian Ingrao reviews the lives of many of these ideologues in his book, *Believe and Destroy, Intellectuals in the SS War Machine*. In his book, we find SS officers like Otto Ohlendorf, Werner Best, Reinhardt Höhn, Franz Albert Six, Wilhelm Spengler, Gustav Adolf Scheel, and Wilhelm Albert, the most outstanding intellectuals in a list of almost a hundred. These intellectuals developed new perspectives in all fields of scientific and humanist theory necessary for the establishment of a new cultural foundation.

> "The time spent by future SS cadres at university [was] an aspect of their social and activist education. But it was also the period of their professional and intellectual training. These young men provide no evidence at all for the clichéd image of the thuggish Nazi activist; they gained entrance to universities, and took – and generally passed – their exams. Nor were they the bad boys of a science that they 'perverted'. The content of the courses they followed proves as much. Knowledge, activism and levels of cultural sophistication: it is in the interaction between these three dimensions that the specific character of these activist intellectuals (or, perhaps better, intellectual activists) can be identified." [15]

---

15 Christian Ingrao. *Believe and Destroy*

Ingrao describes that 80% of these intellectuals entered the SD, the Security Office (*Sicherheitsdienst*) of the SS. In that office, organized by SS General (*SS-Gruppenführer*) Reinhard Heydrich and afterwards led by General Ernst Kaltenbrunner, all the economic, political, racial and cultural plans and theories of the SS were developed. The SD was the great intellectual center of the SS and during its existence did its best to recruit the elite of the universities of the *Reich* for the development of policies and cultural foundations.

The main centers of SS intellectual vigor were the University of Jena, practically monopolized by the SD, the "Herder Institute" of the University of Riga, the University of Posen, the "Wansee Institute", the "SS Academy of Medicine" (*Arztliche Akademie SS*) in Graz, the "Institute for Foreign Research" (*Ausland Wissenschaftlichen*) of the University of Bern, the "Leipzig Office for Intellectual Security" (*Leipzig Schrittumstelle*), and the "National Office of Habitat and Culture" (*Deutsches Lebengebiet*). Within this network of schools, academies and training centers, were the "SS Men's Houses" or "SS Troop House" (*SS-Mannschaftshäuser*), groups made up of SS members studying non-military or political professions in the universities of the *Reich*. The chief of these houses was *SS-Oberführer* Kurt Ellersiek.

Elsewhere, the NS-Worldview was elaborated and developed in the training centers for cadets and leaders of the SS, the ideological training-grounds for political soldiers. These were the "National Policy Studies Centers" or NAPOLA Schools (*Nationalpolitische Erziehungsanstalt*), as well as the ideological training centers of the NSDAP called "Castles of the Order" (*Ordensburg*), with headquarters in Santhofen, Crossinsee, Vogelstand and Marienburg and, the "National Schools for SS Leaders" (*Reichsfuhrerschule*) in locations like Bad Tolz, Branschweig, Possen, Klagenfurt and Prague. By 1942, these centers supervised the research and scientific production which epitomized the National Socialist Worldview.

But the most ambitious project in the preparation of a new intelligentsia was the "NSDAP School of Higher Studies" (*Hohe Schule der NSDAP*). The project, which failed to get past its initial stage, involved the creation of large research and teaching centers which would impart the Worldview exclusively to leaders of the Movement. The philosopher Alfred Bäumler was the first director of this university of Nazism. The "NSDAP School of Higher Studies", even in its earliest beginning, had the active collaboration of SS members and intellectuals who participated as teachers, academics and administrators.

SOURCES OF THE NS-WORLDVIEW

The National Socialist ideology's centers of thought were mostly under the wing of the SS. In that organization, the Nazi Worldview was investigated and given scientific value, mainly through the "SS Education Office" (*SS-Schulungsamt*), headed by SS Lieutenant Colonel (*SS-Obersturmbannführer*) Joachim Caesar, and later by psychologist and SS Lieutenant-general Ludwig Eckstein. This body was fundamental in spreading, organizing, and giving scientific foundation to the National Socialist Worldview. All the materials produced by the Education Office went to the SS Main Office (*SS-Hauptamt*), the most important body in the SS State. There they were approved and issued as official communications to the leaders and officers of the Movement. The Main Office, of SS General (*SS-Obergruppenführer*) Karl Wolff and later led by SS General Maximilian von Herff, was the productive core of SS thought. The Main Office obtained its ideological focus from the Office of the Deputy Staff of the SS Reich Leader" (*Hauptamt Persönlicher Stab Reichsführer-SS*), first led by SS General August Heissmeyer and later by the SS General Gottlob Berger. Everything that emanated from this office carried the *Reichsführer-SS* Himmler's seal of approval.

Official publications, the most important vehicles for the preparation of leaders and instructors, also depended on the Office of Deputy Personnel. Among these publications were instruction and ideological books which began to be published after 1941. Perhaps the most important of these journals was the publication for officers and instructors called *Guidance Notebooks* (*Leitheft*), directed by Ludwig Eckstein, a journal of ideological orientation for the instruction of leaders of the SS. Also important was the journal for the university student's organization of the SS "SS Troop Houses" (*SS-Mannschaftshäuser*), edited by Kurt Ellersiek, *SS-Oberführer* and deputy inspector of the NAPOLA political schools, and the journal of political orientation "Political Service Supplement for SS and Police" (*Beiblatt zum Politischen Dienst für SS und Polizei*). The SS ideology was also spread publicly and massively through the nationally circulated newspaper *The Black Corps* (*Das Schwarze Korps*), edited by journalist and *SS-Hauptsturmführer* Gunter d'Alquen.

Another important body of ideological production was the NS-Education Office (*Reichschulungsamtes der NSDAP*), led by NSDAP education leader (*Reichschulungsleiter*) Otto Gohdes. This "ideological education" type of department was replicated by State entities which were not part of the Movement, especially by the Army. For the ideological orientation of the officers and troops, National Socialism created the "NS-Leaders Team of the Army High Command" (*NS-Führungsstab der Oberkommando der Wehrmacht*), an adjunct department created by Hitler's decree in 1943 and led by General Hermann Reinecke. This department came to include some 47,000 officers who acted as NS-Worldview instructors on the front-lines.

All ideological material not issued by the "SS Main Office", the "NS-Education Office" or by another official National Socialist body, was to be approved by the so-called "Rosenberg Office" (*Amt Rosenberg*). The department was headed by Alfred Rosenberg in his capacity as "Commissioner of the *Führer* for the supervision of all NSDAP education and ideological-intellectual training" an unwieldy name usually shortened to DBFU (*Beauftragten des Führers für die Überwachung der gesamten geistigen und weltanschaulichen Schulung und Erziehung der NSDAP*). The mission of the *Amt Rosenberg* or DBFU was to safeguard and protect the purity of the Nazi ideology, especially by reviewing works published by individuals, even when they were high-ranking officials of the Movement or the State. The National Socialist Worldview's most important ideological purity certification-giving body existed under the direction of the *Amt Rosenberg*, the "Official Examining Commission of the Party for the Protection of National Socialist Writings" or PPK (*Parteiamtliche*

Prüfungskommission zum Schutze des Nationalsozialistischen Schrifttums), led by SS General (*SS-Obergruppenführer*) Philipp Bouhler. It was responsible for creating the "National Bibliography" (*NS-Bibliographie*), certifying the ideological purity of all works intended to convey the Nazi Worldview. The Commission had been created as an appendix to the "*Führer* Chancellery of the NSDAP" by Hitler's order, in order to prevent the distortion of either the Worldview, his writings and speeches, and those of the other *Reich* Leaders. The Commission approved ideological content through printed seals, one indicating that the book in question was approved and included in the Nazi bibliography (*Die Schrift wird in der NS Bibliographie geführt*) and a second seal that approved the content as official ideology without including it in the Nazi bibliography, something which had no relation to ideological purity (*Gegen die Herausgabe dieser Schrift werden seitens der NSDAP keine Bedenken erhoben*). Only books with these seals or with a note indicating that the SS or NSDAP were the reviewing and issuing entity, could be considered as the official ideology of the National Socialist Worldview.

In 1944 an official list of the most important ideological texts regarding diverse subjects was published. "Seven hundred books for the National Socialist Library" (*Siebenhundert Bücher für nationalsozialistische Buchereien*) covered titles and publications with National Socialist content, separated by theme, including warfare, philosophy, history of Nazism, ancient history, politics, science, agriculture, racial science, labor, political enemies, poetry, etc.

NS-Worldview And Ideological Instruction

Establishing the National Socialist Worldview was the joint effort of all the organizations of the Movement. The objective of the Party was to attain political power, then to impose the Worldview on society. Professional associations had to give it scientific rigor. Education and training bodies had to teach it to the population, and cultural organizations were in charge on its dissemination. The SS had to defend it internally during its ideological elaboration. The Armed Forces and later the Waffen SS had the role to defend it from external threats.

The SS was the most committed to the Worldview, and was the institution that dedicated the most space to it in its ideological programmes. For the SS, the Worldview played a hegemonic role in the life of individual members.

> Only the National Socialist Worldview assures us an appropriate kind of life. What is a Worldview? A Worldview is a vision of the world. In a broader sense, it is the culmination of all the thoughts and ideas about the world and the life of a community. Each Worldview is shaped and conditioned by the whole existence of man: race, education, environment and experience. Worldviews are therefore the expressions of human lifeforms and vice versa. National Socialism is a natural Worldview. We have to recall to consciousness everything implied by the following words: struggle for existence, selection, fertility, race, inheritance, environment influence, and development.[16]

For the SS, all other instruction was secondary. Politics, economics, and sociology did not have such a profound meaning in comparison to the laws of existence.

> The foundations of our Worldview are based on the natural *Life-Laws*. The awareness of the importance of the lifelaws has brought new significance to every term. The historical concepts of State will lose their importance. Dogmatic laws are weak compared to nature. A biological legalism determines new limits and relationships.[17]

In the publications and indoctrination courses of the SS it was common to begin with the definitions and meanings of the *Life-Laws*. There was no ideological text that did not define them before moving on to other topics. The laws of struggle, selection, fertility and inheritance were definitively the basis for all the instruction of the Nazi Worldview.

---

16 SS-Hauptamt. *Notebooks for Worldview Teaching*
17 SS-Hauptamt. *Teaching plan for Worldview education of the SS and Police*

The Law of Life

The SS *Notebooks for Worldview Teaching (Handblätter für den Weltanschaulichen Unterricht)*, a collection of 25 volumes edited by the "SS Main Office" to explain the Worldview to the leaders of the Movement were explicit. The first volume, "Only the National Socialist Worldview Assures Us a Correct Type of Life", began with a quotation from *Mein Kampf* which claimed that National Socialism was scientific and therefore unrelated to mystical teachings. The first chapter explained that the Worldview was naturalistic and its fourth chapter taught how struggle was one of the main *Laws of Life*. The second volume, "*Life-Laws, Foundations of our Worldview*," explained this. The text dealt with the *Law of Struggle* for existence (*Kampf ums Dasein*), and the laws of selection, inheritance and fertility. SS-Man and Blood Questions. (*SS-Mann und Blütfrage*) was another SS instruction book explaining the NS-Worldview and the biological foundations implicit therein. Again the text began with the chapter "*Laws of Life*" (*Gesetze des Lebens*). The *Law of Struggle* was explained as the foundation of life. Secondly, the *Law of Fertility* was addressed, which for the text was the foundation of development. Thirdly, the *Law of Selection* explained the basis of evolution and increasing value. "SS Racial Science" (*SS-Rassenkunde*) and "Believe and Fight" (*Glauben und Kämpfen*), two fundamental manuals for the Worldview's teaching, contained identical text when explaining the naturalistic foundation of the Worldview, especially in the chapter "Nature is selection through struggle". The text "Teaching plan for Worldview education in SS and Police" (*Lehrplan für die Weltanschauliche Erhiehung der SS und Polizei*), devoted its entire fourth chapter, *The Vital Foundations of our Worldview*, to explain the same *Laws of Life* as the foundations of a new order.

On the other hand *Racial Policy* (*Rassenpolitik*) also published by the SS-Main Office, summarized the basis of the government's racial policies and reviewed the actions that must be taken in defense of the *Laws of Life*. Among those texts not published by the SS, it is important to note *Why Do We Fight?* (*Wofür Kämpfen Wir?*), was published by the Army and overseen by the *Führer* himself for distribution to all the fighters of the *Reich* during the last stage of the war. Mention must also be made of *Struggle as Life-Law* (*Kampf als Lebensgesetz*), which urged the warriors of the new Europe to defend the *Life-Laws* and the National Socialist Worldview. These texts reviewed the fundamental importance of the principle laws of struggle, selection, inheritance and fertility.

Perhaps due to the character of its political objectives, the National Socialist Party was behind the SS in terms of ideological development and propagation of the Worldview. The official education body of the NSDAP (*Reichschulungsamtes der NSDAP*), through the official ideological manual, or *"Schulungsbrief"*, did however very clearly establish the life-laws as the foundation of its political work.

> The National Socialist recognizes eternal laws. For us, the world is an organic formation, controlled by eternal laws. On the foundations of our Worldview we must build the State and the economy.[18]

A paragon of ideological purity in the Party was Friedrich Schmidt, a High Political Leader (*Hauptbefehlsleiter*) of the NSDAP Indoctrination Division, who revealed in a prologue to Walther Darré's work "National Socialist Racial Policy", the same consciousness of the laws of the Worldview that SS officers had.

The revolutionary philosophy of National Socialism rests in the fact that for the first time in history natural laws have been recognized as valid for mankind. The blood issue, considered as a matter of race and biological laws, determines every plan and every action of government.

NS-WORLDVIEW AND SCIENCE

One of Hitler's major preoccupations during the elaboration of the National Socialist Worldview was to prevent it from becoming a kind of indeterminate philosophy, abandoned to the abstractions of thought. But once the struggle for power was over and he was firmly installed in power, Hitler was able to entrust the mission of elaborating the Worldview with appropriately precise scientific rigor to the Movement

---

18 Otto Gohdes. *Educational Notebooks*

The Law of Life

In the eyes of National Socialism, the *Laws of Life* were part of an order that gave existence to an organic and vitalist foundation of universal character.

> The same laws that govern the course of the stars, which make plants grow and animals fight for life, also govern men. Every man is subject to the inexorable pressure of the *Life-Laws*. Human and natural laws are identical. Those who deviate from these laws perish. Everything is in motion; everything is eternal change, because everything is alive. Who lives according to the laws of nature lives morally.[19]

That is why, for Nazism, all sciences could contribute to the study of these laws. However, the most emphasis was given to the biological sciences, since Man was the focus of Nazi efforts, and biologists were set to work discovering how the Laws were related to human physiology. In this sense, biology was the primary science of the Worldview.

But for Nazism, relegating knowledge of the *Life-Laws* only to the sciences was not enough. Scientific discoveries and knowledge had to be transmitted to the people so that they could be applied in daily life. This was the political mission of National Socialism. Society should keep the *Life-Laws* as a cultural prism, thus conditioning its actions to remain faithful to this natural order. This cultural filter was called "Life-Law Thinking" (*Lebensgesetzlichen denken*), and also biological or organic thinking. In this paradigm, raciology and biology were fundamental since at long last the biological aspect of man was given pride of place in asserting the *Life-Laws*. Out of this way of thinking came so-called Racial Thought (*Rassengedanke*) and Blood Questions (*Blütfrage*). During the Nazi *Reich*, racial research meant the effort to understand the relationship between the *Life-Laws* and man. Thus, raciology was a necessary product of the NS-Worldview.

It was Himmler, contrary to the popular conceptions of him, who began

---

19 Friedrich Oesterle. Everything has its Order. *Guidance Notebooks*, SS-Hauptamt

a period of scientific renaissance and ideological modernization in the Nazi Movement. The SS began along a path of methodological rigor which led the SS cadres to associate with renowned scientists. This path of professionalization did not allow speculation and soon broke from the attempts of some scientists to create so-called "Aryan sciences". The National Socialist Worldview did not rule out observable phenomena and during this process of professionalization it eliminated some of the more eccentric aspects of the philosophy of earlier times.

> The old world has collapsed; the Nordic spirit has opened the door to a new scientific Worldview. As a result of this revolutionary discovery, the Worldview of the medieval church gradually falls apart. We owe this to technological advances, sciences and economics. Copernicus, Kepler, Galileo and other scientists began the battle between modern science and dogma. The Nordic scientific spirit only accepts as true what is in accordance with science and experience. The National Socialist Worldview, based on knowledge of heritability and racial differences, will overcome and surpass ancient beliefs and return the Germanic peoples to their original Worldview. Racial science is based on the most advanced genetics. Nordic scientists are always delving deeper and deeper into the secrets of life and nature. When National Socialism took power in Germany, most citizens could not grasp the revolutionary knowledge of racial science and genetics. The victory of racial thought in such a short time is impressive. Scientific knowledge generally requires decades, even centuries to be accepted in people's thinking. The Worldview that Adolf Hitler developed, based on incontrovertible scientific evidence, has enabled a large part of the population to be persuaded of the correct and decisive nature of racial thought.[20]

The synthesis of the NS-Worldview with biological sciences began with a pact between the SS and the leading biologists and directors of research institutes, such as Eugen Fischer, Otmar von Verschuer and

---

20   SS-Hauptamt. *Racial Policy*

Ernst Rudin. Dr. Arthur Gutt, SS General (*SS-Obergruppenführer*) and high official of the Ministry of the Interior, and SS General Leonardo Conti, head of the National Health Office (*Reichsgesundheitsführer*), who were in charge of coordinating scientific institutes according to Nazi ideology. All those responsible for the Racial Policies of the Movement had to become familiar with these institutes of biological science. Sheila Faith Weiss, author of the book *The Nazi Symbiosis: Human Genetics and Politics in the Third Reich*, investigated this relationship in detail, and the need for National Socialism to base its Worldview on scientific principles.

> It is sometimes argued that all National Socialists were anti-intellectual and opposed to scientific research, but this is a myth... National Socialist policy in this key area should not appear to the world to contradict internationally accepted views on human heredity.[21]

NS-Worldview Symbols

National Socialism's characteristic feature was its use of iconography and symbolism, which served as propaganda tools and self-identification in political struggle. This strategy was very effective at that time and highly suggestive today. But the use of these symbols was framed within the limits of the Nazi Worldview, leaving aside previous interpretations from history, archeology, neo-pagan philosophies and runic mysticism. The symbols of National Socialism made sense only within the framework of the *Life-Laws*.

For National Socialism, the main law of the Worldview was the *Law of Struggle* and its symbol was the swastika. For National Socialism this symbol transcended the cultural boundaries of the Germanic tribes, being the banner of all the branches of the Europid family tree.

> The *Führer* says in *Mein Kampf* that we can see "in the swastika the Aryan man's mission to struggle". The *Führer*'s faith and

---
[21] Sheila Faith Weiss. *Nazi Symbiosis*

will gave birth to the idea and raised the swastika flag, a symbol of life-in-struggle and of future struggles.[22]

The great symbol of Nazism was interpreted with the analogy of a world in movement and constant becoming due to the indefatigable nature of life-as-struggle.

> The Aryan spirit does not know a perfect world. The world is more like a wheel that turns on itself, symbolized by the swastika.[23]

In addition to the swastika, Nazism used the so-called runes, symbols of the Germanic culture whose original names and meanings did not survive to modern times. And while philologists, archeologists, and neo-pagan mystics gave them different names and interpretations, Nazism provided them with another meaning according to the laws of its Worldview.

Within the Nazi hierarchy, the leader of warriors and instructor of the Worldview and its Law of perpetual struggle generally displayed the *Struggle Rune* ↑ (*Kampfrune*) as an insignia. The *Struggle Rune*, known by neo paganism as the *Tyr* rune and by philologists as *Tiwaz*, was used as a badge by all NSDAP leader-instructors, as well as by the SS training department's instructors, who were responsible for military and political instruction. The *Struggle Rune* appeared on decorations for bravery and leadership in combat. SS troops who fell in combat were commonly buried under the *Struggle Rune* symbol.

The warrior who took part in the struggle for existence took as his symbol the *ray of victory*, called the *Victory Rune* ⚡(*Sieg rune*). The SS used it as a double symbol because of its initials *Schutz-Staffel*. Meanwhile the heroes who sacrificed themselves in combat were symbolized by the *Sacrifice Rune* ᛂ (*Opfer rune*). The commemoration ceremonies of the fallen in the Movement during the

---

22　*Struggle as Life Law.* NS Leadership Staff of the High Command of the Armed Forces.

23　Fritz Reich. *Birth and End of the World in the Aryan Myth*, Guidance Notebooks, SS-Hauptamt

The Law of Life

years of political struggle were adorned with this symbol. The zeal and enthusiasm of the militants was represented with the *Enthusiasm Rune* ↜ (*Eif rune*). Rudolf Hess, the *Führer's* lieutenant, took it as an ensign, as well as many other members of Hitler's adjunct staff.

The *Law of Selection* and the *Law of Inheritance* were symbolized with the *Blood and Soil Rune* ᛟ (*Blüt und Boden rune*), a symbol that the neo-pagans knew as *Odal*. The offices specializing in selection, and elite groups, were identified with this ancestral symbol. It was used by the two great archetypes of Nazi selection, the peasant or rural family and the elite SS clans. The hereditary farm or *Erbhof*, a title given to peasants' lands of certified Germanic tradition, had on its main entryway this distinctive symbol of selection. It was also used on the uniforms of SS members who were affiliated with the "Race and Settlements" or RuSHA (*Rasse-und Siedlungshauptamt-SS*). It was also as the mark of the office concerned with the cultural heritage, the Ancestors Heritage Office (*Ahnenerbe*).

The *Law of Fertility*, was distinguished with the symbol called the *Life Rune* ᛉ (*Leben rune*), known to the Neo-pagans as *Man* and to philologists and historians as *Algiz*. The *Life Rune* was used as a symbol of all fertility and health-promoting entities, such as the German Women's Association (*Deutsches Frauenwerk*) and the Source of Life organization (*Lebensborn*), a body that administered orphanages, adoption programs, maternity homes and financial assistance to single mothers. The symbol was also used in the anti-tobacco crusade of the *Reich*. The *Life Rune* was used by all sections and sub-sections of Movement and State agencies devoted to health. It was also a very common and popular graphic used in the production of ideological material. Instructional manuals frequently portrayed it as a symbol of fertility, procreation, and community preservation. Other runes associated with fertility, although used to a lesser extent, were the *Harvest Rune* ᛇ (*Erntesegen rune*) and the *Health Rune* (*Heil rune*).

Enemies of the NS-Worldview

For National Socialism abandoning the *Life-Laws* would bring serious degenerative effects, even extinction, thus its violent conviction when confronting its Worldview's enemies.

> Our planet moved through space for millions of years, uninhabited by men, and at some future date may easily begin to do so again, if men should forget that wherever they have reached a superior level of existence, it was not as a result of following the ideas of crazy visionaries but by acknowledging and rigorously observing the iron laws of Nature.[24]

The enemies of the National Socialist Worldview were identified from the beginning by Hitler as all those groups and organizations that violated the *Life-Laws*. In this group were included all metaphysical, materialist, humanist and rationalist ideologies which put man above natural laws, idealizing man as a creature that could be removed from the order ruling over all organisms of the earth. It was in this sense that Hitler designated Judaism as the main enemy of the Nazi Worldview. For the *Führer*, the European Jews were the most dangerous enemies of the Worldview, since, even though they were conscious of the reality of the *Life Laws*, they created false ideologies aimed to confuse the other nations of the earth.

> It is no accident that it is always primarily the Jew who tries and succeeds in planting such mortally dangerous modes of thought in our people. He knows his customers too well not to realize that they gratefully let themselves be swindled by any goldbrick salesman who can make them think he has found a way to play a little trick on Nature, to make the hard, inexorable struggle for existence superfluous...That is one of the results of our defective education, which deprives young people of their natural instincts...All such ideas, which have nothing to do with cold logic as such, but represent mere manifestations of feeling, such as ethical and moral conceptions, etc.[25]

---

24   Hitler. *Mein Kampf*
25   Hitler. *Mein Kampf*

The struggle against the enemies of the NS-Worldview was constant and became a priority after Hitler came to power. The SS intelligence chief, SS General Reinhard Heydrich, reported in a 1936 text entitled *The Transformation of our Struggle*, that although the initial struggle was basically against political opponents, the second phase was aimed at intellectual enemies, those organizations and individuals that in a veiled way sowed ideas contrary to the *Life-Laws*. According to Heydrich, the Worldview was largely unknown even to some Nazis, militants who were mistaken in thinking that their enemies had been defeated in the political struggle.

The *Reich's* political machinery promptly instituted a police system which had sections specially designed for neutralising the enemies of the Worldview. The intelligence agency of the SS, the SD, in its internal section led by SS Colonel Hermann Behrends and then SS General Franz Six, established an entire investigation department exclusively centered on the enemies of the Worldview, the so-called "Central Section II: , Investigation of Enemies" (*Zentralabteilung II / 1: Gegnererforschung*), under the direction of SS Captain Erich Ehrlinger. This section was divided into two research sections. One focused on political enemies (*Politische Gegner*) of the Worldview, like Marxism, liberalism and conservativeism (*liberaler und konservativer Gegner*), as well as right-wing movements (*Rechtsbewegung*). The other section focused on the Worldview's non-political enemies (*Weltanschauliche Gegner*). This had among its sub-sections Masonry, managed by SS Second Lieutenant Dieter Wisliceny; International Judaism, under the direction of second lieutenant SS Herbert Hagen and Churches and Spiritual Organizations including Occultist Movements", a section led by SS Major Albert Hartl. During the war the enemies of the NS-Worldview were not only individuals and organizations but countries.

> World War II is mainly a confrontation between worldviews. The political, military and economic measures adopted in its course are only the attempts of each side to shape the world according to its beliefs.[26]

---

26 SS-Hauptamt. *The Defense of Europe.*

England was cataloged as the embodiment of a puritan Worldview with plutocratic, imperialistic objectives. The United States was cataloged as the heir of the English Worldview in a more materialistic form and the Soviet Union as the incarnation of the Marxist Worldview of counter-selective collectivism.

Despite the Nazi conviction that war could have been avoided if it had not been for the warmongering campaign of prominent Jews in the governments of England, the United States and the Soviet Union, once the conflict erupted, the NS-Worldview's elaborators soon understood the world conflagration as a decisive struggle between the National Socialist and Jewish Worldviews. The latter, according to Nazism, was rooted in the Old Testament and sustained via a mixture of mystical-religious teachings together with a little-noticed code of racial preservation. In this sense it would seem that National Socialism was firmly convinced that the Nazi and Jewish worldviews were two visions of the world rooted in the laws of existence but irreconcilably antagonistic in their spiritual aims.

> The Old Testament, the Torah, the Talmud and the Schulchan-Aruch are in historical and ideological terms a metaphysical-structural unity. But if one reads the Old Testament, especially the books of Moses, the book of Ezra and the Mehira, one can verify the firmness of the Life and Blood Laws found therein. Conveyed through religious laws arranged in an extraordinarily intelligent manner are the arguments that transform the Jews into God's chosen people, in addition to giving them the feeling of supremacy over the rest of humanity.[27]

---

27 Army Personnel Office. *Why Do We Fight?*.

The Law of Struggle

According to National Socialism, the most important Life-Law was the *Law of Struggle* (*Kampfgesetz*). In this sense the National Socialist Worldview was heir of the Indo-European thought of Heraclitus and his world of perpetual strife, called *Polemos*. The National Socialist Worldview was also the intellectual heir of Nietzsche's world-in-eternal-becoming and universe-as-an-agonal-game.

"Life as struggle" was a conviction Hitler acquired during the years of the Great War and voiced until his death in speeches, writings and conversations. In World War I an unknown facet of life was revealed to that young artist, as he began to understand the natural order behind the ideological veil of modern cultural life. The experience of life´s characteristic dynamic as struggle was later dubbed *heroic realism,* the ability to see the world without any idealism.

> It was with feelings of pure idealism that I set out for the front in 1914. Then I saw men falling around me in the thousands. Thus I learnt that life is a cruel struggle, and has no other object but the preservation of the species.[28]

Understanding life as struggle gave the young Hitler an idea of the growing disconnection between cultural discourse and the natural order. For Hitler, the *Life-Laws* and especially the Struggle Law, were the true order of nature, therefore, man should not abstract himself from that reality. In Hitler's eyes, all philosophies and ideologies which diverted men from these laws were nothing more than naiveté and self-delusion, resulting in the complete alienation of mankind from the natural order.

> The real truth is, that not only has man failed to overcome

---
28 Hitler. *Table Talk*

Nature in any sphere whatsoever, but that at best he has merely succeeded in getting hold of and lifting a tiny corner of the enormous veil which she has spread over her eternal mysteries and secrets. He never invents anything; all he can do is to discover something. He does not master nature, but has only come to be master of those living beings who have not gained the knowledge he has arrived at by penetrating into some of Nature's laws and mysteries.

Millions thoughtlessly parrot this Jewish nonsense...that they themselves represent a kind of *conquerer* of Nature.

Man must not fall into the error of thinking that he was ever meant to become lord and master of Nature. A lopsided education has helped to encourage that illusion. Man must realize that a fundamental law of necessity reigns throughout the whole realm of Nature and that his existence is subject to the law of eternal struggle and strife. He will then feel that there cannot be a separate law for mankind in a universe in which planets and suns follow their orbits, where the strong are always the masters of the weak and where the latter must obey or be destroyed. Man must also submit to the eternal principles of this supreme wisdom. He may try to understand them but he can never free himself from their sway.

Man's effort to build up something that contradicts the iron logic of Nature brings him into conflict with those principles to which he himself exclusively owes his very existence.[29]

For Hitler, the modern ideologies restraining man from these laws were only damaging the foundation and substance of his vital totality, producing an abyss between intellect and nature, a duality between mind and flesh. For Hitler, the spirit and all the mental and psychological phenomena which had produced the abstractions of Western thought were based in nature, therefore inhered in flesh and

---

29   Hitler. *Mein Kampf*

blood. Keeping them within these boundaries produced progress and preservation. To remove them from there meant human decay.

> Whatever is made of flesh and blood can never escape the laws that condition its development. As soon as the human intellect believes itself to be above that, the real substance that is the bearer of the spirit is destroyed.[30]

In Hitler's Worldview the *Law of Struggle* supported all aspects of life; therefore there was no possibility of a life outside struggle. For Hitler, without struggle there was no life.

> He who would live must fight. He who does not wish to fight in this world, where permanent struggle is the law of life, has not the right to exist. Such a statement may sound hard, but, after all, that is how the matter really stands. Yet far harder is the lot of him who believes that he can overcome Nature, and thus in reality insults her. Distress, misery, and disease are her rejoinders.[31]

In his *Second Book*, struggle was not only described as a law for all living beings, but also as the characteristic feature of a Universal Order. Struggle, for Hitler, was not just an evolutionary, biological tool, but an essential law of creation.

> The history of the world in the ages when humans did not yet exist was initially a representation of geological occurrences. The clash of natural forces with each other, the formation of a habitable surface on this planet, the separation of water and land, the formation of the mountains, the plains, and the seas... Later, with the emergence of organic life, and the appearance and disappearance of its thousandfold forms. Man himself finally becomes visible very late, and from that...

> This development is characterized by the never-ending battle of humans against animals and also against humans themselves.

---

[30] Hitler. *Second Book*
[31] Hitler. *Mein Kampf*

> Finally, out of the unclear tangle of individual beings, formations rise—families, tribes, peoples, states. The portrayal of their genesis and dissolution is but the replication of an eternal struggle for survival.[32]

In Hitler's ethics, this eternal struggle preserved the Universe in a state of good health.

> All nature is a tremendous struggle between strength and weakness, the eternal victory of the strong over the weak. If it were not so, nature would be nothing but putrefaction.[33]

For Nazism, a static and calm existence did not allow for preservation, only existence in movement, struggle and eternal becoming ensured a constant overcoming and the advances necessary for life's development.

> In eternal struggle humanity has grown, in eternal peace it would perish.[34]

For Nazism, the world was in constant strife and an ever-threatening environment forced each generation to fight for its own preservation. The struggle had no end, and if one generation attempted to placate the spirit of struggle, to retreat from the need to fight, the efforts of previous generations would be for naught.

> Every people has an obligation to take care of itself. Every generation has the mission of settling its accounts for itself. Do not think that we are going to take everything away from the future. No and no, we do not want to educate our youth to become life's dirty parasite and to cowardly enjoy what others have created. No, what you wish to possess you will have to win again; you will have to throw yourself once more into fight.

---

32 Hitler. *Second Book*
33 Hitler. *1923 Speech*
34 Hitler quoted in *The Road to the NSDAP*. SS-Hauptamt.

We want to educate men for this. We do not want to infuse in them from the beginning the false theory that this struggle is unnatural or unworthy of man, on the contrary, we want to instill in them the idea that this struggle is the eternal condition for selection, that without the eternal struggle there would be no men on the earth. No, what we do now, we do for ourselves! [35]

For Hitler struggle was a necessary prerequisite of life. Struggle was the generative principle of existence.

A nation can prosper only if it does not forget for a second, that nothing is given in life, but that struggle is the father of all things.[36]

THE FATHER OF ALL THINGS

Hitler's phrase concerning struggle as father of all things was inspired by the pre-Socratic philosopher Heraclitus. This Greek thinker called life-as-struggle *Polemos*, strife. Heraclitus was the Greek philosopher who wrote most of the meditations regarding life as a struggle.

Conflict *(Polemos)* is the father *(Pater)* and the king *(Basileus)* of all things *(Panta)*; and some he has made gods and some men, some slaves and some free.[37]

In this worldview, the union of all entities in the universe formed a chaotic and undifferentiated mass called *Hen*, the "One", in other words, the gatherer of everything. *Hen* was pure existence, a shapeless being. It was a seeming chaos, an undifferentiated mass. Only the struggle, *Polemos*, allowed individual beings to be extracted from that undifferentiated chaos, hence the diversity of the world. This is what the Greeks called *Panta* or "the many." These entities obtained their appearances relative to the differences between them.

---

35   Hitler. Speech at the Congress of the German Labor Front. Berlin, 1933
36   SS-Hauptamt. Hitler quoted in *Guide for the Celebration of the Führer's Birthday.*
37   Heraclitus. *Fragment 53*

This differentiation was possible thanks to partition, a consequence of struggle. *Polemos* was the father who forced the "One" to manifest his multiple traits, since conflict could not arise in a unified being (*Hen*). According to Heraclitus, conflict was only possible as long as there were adversaries, consequently the multiplicity of the world (*Panta*) was necessary.

Polemos divided and individualized, forcing *Hen* to become *Panta*. Struggle forced chaos to take on multiple forms, while this division created boundaries and delimited boundaries according to specific contours and shapes. In man, this organizing capacity was produced through the intellect, the *Logos*, which ordered, differentiated and schematized. This allowed reality to be perceived as a multiplicity of concrete entities and for man to recognize "*gods as gods and men as men*", according to Heraclitus.

For Heraclitus, *Polemos* not only created entities, but also allowed for their preservation. Therefore these entities permanently fought to keep their character, constancy and appearance, in a dynamic equilibrium, since they gained vitality on the one hand and lost it on the other, jeopardizing their individual existence. Nietzsche was influenced by this Heraclitean doctrine. In his vitalist philosophy living beings constantly lost biological dynamism due to cellular fatigue, as energy burned and even as memories faded. On the other hand, feeding, breathing, and even mental exercises compensated for that loss of vitality by extracting from the environment and assimilating what was necessary to keep functioning. Nietzsche observed that man permanently faces loss and gain, defeat and conquest; life is a matter of existing or disappearing in an eternal struggle, just as all other creatures in the world do. Nietzsche called this instinctive function the *Will to Power*, which tended to constantly recover lost vitality.

According to the pre-western thinkers, struggle was common to all beings, and it was considered the essence of the universe, that which modern philosophers call "Being". That is the reason why Heraclitean thought considered a shapeless existence, *Hen*, the "One", as having the same existential essence as *Panta*, "the many forms". For

The Law of Struggle

Heraclitus, a dualism did not exist between the essence of beings and their appearance, or between gods and nature. In that sense, struggle allowed man to exist and also to preserve his existence. As stated by the ancient Greeks, *Polemos* belongs to us, since we ourselves are conflict.

For Nietzsche and the Nazis, an abyss was irremediably opened at the dawn of the West with the philosophy of Socrates and later with the Platonic myth of the cave, the myth of a new Being for Western Indo-Europeans. Plato constructed an analogy where the life of man on earth was equivalent to living inside a cave. The inhabitants of the interior of the Platonic cave perceived shadows projected onto the inner wall by outer beings. Among these shadows the cavern dwellers built their own idea of reality. In this analogy, the natural world, corresponding to the interior of the cavern, was only a poor imitation of the real world, outside the cave, representing transcendent and perennial ideas, the real essence of those illusory shadows.

With this myth, man's essence was no longer associated with nature and was pushed up towards a transcendental plane. This was the birth of metaphysical dualism. The Ideal emerged in that moment as a new truth, outside of nature. In this myth, man and the world became only illusory shadows of something real. The father of all things was thought of from that moment on as a trans-mundane entity, perfect, without error or defeat. The essence of beings became an ideal, an eternal and moral archetype, good and perfect in itself. Metaphysical essence was thought immobile, unchangeable, incapable of fighting, a conservative entity that was largely unattainable, as well as transcendent, alien and improper to man.

At the historical moment at which the culture of life-as-struggle decayed and became Western dualist culture, values became universal substances whose essence was above natural reality. Jaan Puhvel, a scholar of Indo-European history, called this phenomenon *Pandemonium*. In this process —which occurred around the sixth century BC across many Indo-European cultures at the same time— the gods were transformed into representatives of eternal good and evil. The reformer Zarathustra created Mazdaism—dualism— by demonizing the *devas* of the sacred texts of the *Avesta*. The same thing happened in ancient India with the *Rigveda*, which demonized the *asuras*. At this time, the Orphic mysteries and Pythagorean speculations arose, placing the origin of human vitality in supernatural beings, while Socrates and Plato conceptualized the theory of eternal ideas.

At this time Being in the West ceased to be struggle, the essence that united all of existence. Being was placed in the sphere of eternal ideas beyond man and nature. For this reason, some began to worship it as something distant and mysterious, while others ended up forgetting it, since it was separated from nature. The adoration of this metaphysical Being was the foundation of the European middle ages. On the other hand, neglecting Being is the pillar of modern nihilism. With this new cultural basis, western man assumed that all entities had two essences. On one hand, the natural or physical substance. And on the other, the ideal or metaphysical essence. In the West, the transmundane essence has been thought of as soul, unconscious, spirit, pure reason, or God. Thus, Western man has been fragmented in two, into a dualism of essences. For the NS Worldview, to overcome this dualism meant to overcome the West, but the way of overcoming it had to be radical, otherwise it would be fictitious and unattainable. Such were the attempts of many transcendental schools and religions which sought to overcome the double essence of man, but which, rather than leaving natural essence as man's sole foundation, held up metaphysical essence as the ultimate reality of beings.

Nietzschean Legacy

The West's metaphysical dualism was not present in the Heraclitean worldview. According to the great German philosopher Martin Heidegger, one of Heraclitus' most brilliant interpreters, this pre-Socratic philosopher was a non-metaphysical thinker, not even a pre-metaphysician, since that would mean a tendency to Western metaphysics. For Heidegger, to think like Heraclitus required a great effort.

You do not think metaphysically any longer. Heraclitus does not think metaphysically... To stop thinking metaphysically is more difficult than to not be metaphysical at all.[38]

But as Heidegger observed, renouncing the Western cultural legacy was not something based on a rational decision.

> We cannot reject Metaphysics like we reject an opinion. In no way can it be left behind as a useless doctrine which one no longer believes in. It would be futile to pretend that, because we sense the end of Metaphysics, we are already above it. Since Metaphysics, even when overtaken, does not disappear.[39]

According to Heidegger, a return to pre-metaphysical thinking would be impossible, but one could possibly come close to it if one took into account that the product would necessarily turn out to be something new. For Heidegger, overcoming dualistic metaphysics was possible from the moment Nietzsche transcribed into words this primordial tradition, since *"until the arrival of Nietzsche it had been preserved, but not spoken"*.

Nietzsche was the first to notice the damage and physiological decline resulting from the weight of the Western cultural legacy. His vocation made him into the prophet of vitalist regeneration in the West, connecting him directly to the work of the Nazis. Nietzsche clearly stated that the West had been founded on a worldview that promoted ideologies that hated life and rejected life's laws. For Nietzsche, these Western ideologies had replaced the laws of existence with doctrines that praised the static, the saturated and the perennial.

> Those things which mankind has hitherto pondered seriously are not even realities, merely imaginings, more strictly speaking lies from the bad instincts of sick, in the profoundest sense injurious natures... to deprive of value the only world which exists – so as to leave over no goal, no reason, no task for our earthly reality!

---

38   Martin Heidegger. *Heraclitus Seminar*
39   Martin Heidegger. *Introduction to Metaphysics*

The concept 'soul', 'spirit', finally even 'immortal soul', invented so as to despise the body, so as to make it sick – 'holy' – so as to bring to all the things in life which deserve serious attention, the questions of nutriment, residence, cleanliness, weather, a horrifying frivolity! Instead of health 'salvation of the soul'... All questions of politics, the ordering of society, education have been falsified down to their foundations because the most injurious men have been taken for great men – because contempt has been taught for the 'little' things, which is to say for the fundamental affairs of life... What is the purpose of those lying concepts, the ancillary concepts of morality 'soul', 'spirit', 'free will', 'God', if it is not the physiological ruination of mankind?... When one directs seriousness away from self-preservation, enhancement of bodily strength, when one makes of greensickness an ideal, of contempt for the body 'salvation of the soul', what else is it but a recipe for décadence?[40]

The goal of Nietzschean philosophy was to use the essence of the Heraclitean worldview to negate the path the West had followed, thus producing a turnaround that would establish the foundation of a new era of Being. In a meaningful irony, Nietzsche had Zarathustra, the great Metaphysical dualist, retract his old error. In his book *Thus Spoke Zarathustra* he made the very founder of Mazdaist dualism repent for adopting ideas foreign to the Indo-European essence and thus bringing defect and cultural annihilation to that people. *Thus Spoke Zarathustra* could just as well have been *Thus spoke Socrates* or *Plato*, the confession of cultural crime, a testimony invented by Nietzsche in order to rectify that error with a new gospel which annulled the previous one. Wolfgang Schultz, a Nazi philosopher of culture, stated that a clear sign that someone had not understood Nietzsche's message was to say that Nietzsche's Zarathustra was a *tribute* to the historical Zarathustra, a testimony of neo-Mazdean faith.

The Nietzschean *Zarathustra* has little more than a name in common with the historical Zarathustra. In a letter to Erwin

---

[40] Nietzsche. *Ecce Homo*

The Law of Struggle

Rohdel he tells him that his Zarathustra is his own creation, without precedent, without precursor, and without peer. This is completely correct.[41]

Thus Spoke Zarathustra was written as a Nietzschean sarcasm, a canto of modern anti-dualism delivered by a dualist of antiquity.

> I have not been asked, as I should have been asked, what the name Zarathustra means in precisely my mouth, in the mouth of the first immoralist: for what constitutes the tremendous uniqueness of that Persian in history is precisely the opposite of this. Zarathustra was the first to see in the struggle between good and evil the actual wheel in the working of things: the translation of morality into the realm of metaphysics, as force, cause, end-in-itself, is his work. But this question is itself at bottom its own answer. Zarathustra created this most fateful of errors, morality: consequently he must also be the first to recognize it.[42]

Heraclitean thinking had a major influence on Nietzsche. For him the pre-classical or pre-Socratic Greek tradition contained the clearest vestiges of the original thinking of life-as-struggle which grounded his vitalist and hierarchical doctrine. For Nietzsche, ideas coming from other Indo-European peoples had brought much more fragmented and decadent cultural elements.

> It is a wonderful idea, welling up from the purest strings of Hellenism, the idea that strife embodies the everlasting sovereignty of strict justice, bound to everlasting laws. Only a Greek was capable of finding such an idea to be the fundament of a cosmology; it is Hesiod's good Eris transformed into the cosmic pronciple; it is the contest-idea of the Greek individual and the Greek state, taken from the gymnasium and the palaestra, from the artist's agon, from the contest between political parties and between cities— all transformed into universal application

---

41 Wolfgang Schultz. *The Zarathustra of Nietzsche and the Historical Zarathustra*
42 Nietzsche. *Ecce Homo*

so that now the wheels of the cosmos turn on it.[43]

It is no surprise then, as Alfred Bäumler, the most important Nazi philosopher, points out, to find in Heraclitus one of the Nietzsche's greatest influences.

> Heraclitus, in whose vicinity in general I feel warmer and more well than anywhere else. Affirmation of transitoriness and destruction... affirmation of antithesis and war... in this I must in any event recognize what is most closely related to me. [44]

For Nietzsche, in *Polemos* there was no dualism and the forces in conflict maintained the struggle eternally, without final synthesis, without a teleological end, only perpetual strife as an agonal game of forces which were equivalent in essence, dedicated to the eternal dance of battle and the eternal creation of forms and appearance.

> The strife of the opposites gives birth to all that comes-to-be; the definite qualities which look permanent to us express but the momentary ascendency of one partner. But this by no means signifies the end of the war; the contest endures in all eternity. Everything that happens, happens in accordance with this strife, and it is just in the strife that eternal justice is revealed.[45]

For Nietzsche, to create *form* (*Gestalt*) was the expression of life, like eternal combat, like the *Will to Power*. The sword of the warrior divided and gave appearance, it extracted form from the undifferentiated. In Nietzsche's ethics the warrior was essentially a creative artist.

> There is in us a power to order, simplify, falsify, artificially distinguish... The form counts as something enduring and therefore more valuable; but the form has merely been invented by us.[46]

---

43 Nietzsche. *Philosophy in the Tragic Age of the Greeks*
44 Nietzsche. *Ecce Homo*
45 Nietzsche. *Philosophy in the Tragic Age of the Greeks*
46 Nietzsche. *The Will to Power*

The Law of Struggle

For Nietzsche, the essence of life was not expressed in the fixed but rather the opposite, its common expression was change and becoming. Each being fought to maintain itself, although in the end it was hopelessly defeated in eternal combat. Struggle, then, was not only the creator of beings, but it was also presented as the way to preserve them.

In the Heraclitean worldview, what allowed being in a stable world was the ability to fight and to limit the chaos of non-form, of non-being. Heidegger called this ability to coagulate becoming," Nietzsche called it "schematizing chaos."

> Not "to know" but to schematize—to impose upon chaos as much regularity and form as our practical needs require.[47]

For Nietzsche to fight, to create limits, to confront, to differentiate, to schematize, to organize, to create appearance and form, were not only human actions, but mankind's *essential* action. This action resulted in a stable world, *"the practical necessities for our preservation."*

Nietzsche's "transmutation of all values" was to initiate the return of the Indo-European values, which, unlike "Western values", accepted becoming, and built its culture, ethics and morals on becoming, on change and conflict. This allowed the creative capacity to develop that made the world moldable to human will. The new Nietzschean value system did not attach the same boundless importance as the West did to the fixed, the archetype, the thing-in-itself and eternal beings, concepts that have molded religion, science, and culture and sustained the eternal Western search for truth. Nietzsche intended *"To return fluidity to the world, to transform the belief that things are in such a way, into the will to say that a thing must become so"*. The Nietzschean project sought to return to the moving Being of Greek culture, to end with the Western fixed Being and its transcendental projection. Being, for Nietzsche, was constant change, perpetual conquest and defeat, since nature was never static.

---

47   Nietzsche. *The Will to Power*

However, this realistic attitude, which understood the dynamics of a world in struggle and movement, did not mean falling into nihilistic despair, where reality was understood as an illusion. The will to fight in Nietzsche did not reach a paranoid suspicion about everything, since it acted in the end under rigid boundaries and limits given by nature and its laws. And while these limits left a broad spectrum for the creation of new possibilities, they also posited a final terrain, impossible to transcend. The Nietzschean warrior fought, and through his action created new realities that became the foundations for the development of life.

The struggle of the Nietzschean warrior was not based on abstraction, skepticism, pessimism or subjective relativism, but on natural laws that framed its action and that determined safe limits that would allow for the development of objective truths, scientific ideas and cultural traditions. For Nietzsche to give "Being" to "becoming" and appearance to the perceptive chaos did not mean to fall into a disintegrating and destructive attitude but on the contrary, it was an attitude that invited constant creation, always with a view toward the conscious construction of solid bases for progress, culture, and tradition:

"Art as the will to overcome becoming, as 'eternalization,' but shortsighted, depending on the perspective: repeating in miniature, as it were, the tendency of the Whole. 'Being' as appearance; reversal of values; appearance was that which conferred value"[48].

NIETZSCHE PROPHET OF THE NS-WORLDVIEW

For the philosopher and Nazi leader Alfred Bäumler, National Socialism was to pick up the banner of the Nietzschean project of transmutation of values and with it to initiate a true revolution that transcended the political order.

> When we see the youth under the banner of the swastika, we remember Nietzsche and his last meditations, where this youth

---
48   Nietzsche. *The Will to Power*

was first demanded. And if today we shout *Heil Hitler!* to this youth, at the same time we salute Friedrich Nietzsche.[49]

Hand in hand with Bäumler, Nietzsche became the prophet of the Nazi Worldview. And this was not a niche interest, but almost a State policy.

Although the real influence of Nietzsche on Hitler is little documented, what is certain is that the *Führer* considered him as one of the greatest German thinkers, read him widely — especially during his Vienna years, as stated by his friend August Kubizek, supported his official diffusion and allowed himself to be presented publicly as an admirer of the philosopher.

> In the Great Hall of the Linz Library are the busts of Kant, Schopenhauer and Nietzsche, the greatest of our thinkers, in comparison with whom the British, the French and the Americans have nothing to offer.... it is Schopenhauer who annihilated the pragmatism of Hegel... Schopenhauer's pessimism, which springs partly, I think, from his own line of philosophical thought and partly from subjective feeling and the experiences of his own personal life, has been far surpassed by Nietzsche.[50]

The SS, meanwhile, adopted him as a secular saint and all the important philosophers of National Socialism dedicated themselves to the study of Nietzsche.

The most important philosopher of Nazism, Alfred Bäumler, based practically all his work on Nietzsche. This was also the time of Heidegger's most intense interest in the subject, on which he gave important seminars, not without controversy, during the war. On the other hand, Richard Oehler, member of the Nazi Party and one of the earliest scholars of Nietzsche, linked him to the National Socialist destiny in his book *Nietzsche and the Germanic Destiny*, a text that

---
49 Alfred Bäumler. *Nietzsche and National Socialism*
50 Hitler. *Table Talk*

exalted Hitler as the great contemporary Nietzschean. Also important was his early work *Nietzsche and His Relationship With Pre-Socratic Philosophy*, one of the earliest studies that clarified the Heraclitean influence on the German philosopher. His brother Max Oehler, an Army officer and another early member of the Nazi Party, was the director of the Nietzsche Archive after the death of the philosopher's sister, Elisabeth Foster-Nietzsche. During National Socialism, the archives under his care were opened to the public and students. The Oehlers were cousins of the Nietzsches and dedicated all their efforts to maintaining a close relationship between the Nietzschean legacy and the Nazi Movement.

Heinrich Härtle, philosopher of the Party and the SS, studied Nietzsche's anti-idealism for its application in ideological diffusion. For Härtle;

> only a conscious National Socialist can fully understand Nietzsche. It should be noted that Nietzsche's affinity with National Socialism is greater than the historical-political effect he has had so far. The political vision of Nietzsche is tremendous. In any case, its influence is not political, but in the order of ideological values. His philosophical arguments contain fragments of National Socialism, he is the prophet of National Socialism.[51]

Nietzsche was also designated as a prophet of National Socialism by Claus Schrempf, philosopher, SS officer and collaborator on the ideological manuals of the SS, the *Guidance Notebooks* (*Leitheft*).

> Critic and prophet at the same time, Nietzsche points to the decadence that threatens his contemporaries, dumbfounded by the drunkenness of progress, but at the same time attacks the pessimists who let themselves be overcome by despair, believing in decadence, presenting to them a vision of a future full of luminous colors. Nietzsche appears as the messenger

---

51 Heinrich Härtle. *Nietzsche and National Socialism*

of life with an enthusiasm for everything that makes a man's life worth living, which makes him strong and proud, that is, aristocratic.[52]

Of the same opinion was the doctor in philosophy and Nietzsche specialist, the SS Official Gerhart Schinke, one of the heads of the SS Office of Education (*SS-Schulungamt*). Also Kurt Eggers, a young SS officer (*SS-Obersturmführer*), journalist and writer, who dedicated his life to rhapsodizing heroism, pointed to Nietzsche as the father of the warrior spirit of the new National Socialist man. Eggers' popular books inspired an entire generation with the Nietzschean legacy and their insistence on facing life in a realistic and heroic way, facing nature and leaving aside abstractions and idealisms.

> Friedrich Nietzsche is the most daring thinker of our race. He was the first to have the courage to think in depth the warlike and virile thoughts that move our hearts. In spite of a pacifist and bourgeois environment, that solitary man celebrated the dangerous life and made the decision to be a fighter. His example inspires us to recognize life as it is, without slogans, without pity, with a need for truth. The thinker who can think deeply has always pulled aside this veil. He is the warrior who moves in the world of hostility, defying appearances. Evade this reality or affirm it; that is the decisive thing. Truth or lie.[53]

HERACLITUS' VISION OF THE WORLD

Life as a struggle was the great cultural value and political narrative of National Socialism. Commonly thought by postwar historiography as a projection of Nazi aggressiveness, the law of eternal struggle was a cultural foundation that had its roots in the Nietzsche's revaluation and revival of the Heraclitean legacy. Hitler cited Heraclitus as the foundation of his doctrine of perpetual struggle and the Nazi philosophers were very clear in linking this cultural foundation with

---

52 Claus Schrempf. *Nietzsche, the Prophet*, in *Guidance Notebooks*, SS-Hauptamt
53 Kurt Eggers. *Hostility*

the Greek tradition. Life as struggle was consciously taken from the deepest Indo-European tradition by philosophers such as Nietzsche and his revaluation of the Heraclitean worldview.

Heidegger in his Nazi period, a stage in his philosophy very different from his later existentialism, understood that with National Socialism one entered a different cultural epoch.

> In order to really understand the phrase "struggle is the father and preserver of all things", we need a consciousness of the existence of man and people different from the one we had last year before the rise of National Socialism.[54]

The question of Being in those years of Heidegger's Nazism fell completely under Hitler's influence. For Heidegger, the forgetting of Being was solved by the prior inception, Being-as-strife:

> But what does [the essence of beings] really consist of?... The question itself resonates in our existence, since it received its fundamental orientation through the inception of Greek philosophy. ...If we harken back to this Greek inception... we must grasp that our existence, with all its progress and achievements, lags behind as measured against the inception— and has run off course and lost itself.

> When we... hearken back to the voices of the great inception... to perceive the primordial laws of our Germanic ethnicity... we can hear that saying which gives the first and the decisively great answer to our question about what the essence of beings consists in and how it essences: War is both the father of all things and the king of all things, and on the one hand it shows forth the gods, on the other, human beings; on the one hand it makes slaves, and on the other hand, the free. Struggle does not just allow each being to go forth into what it is, it does not just direct and control the emergence of beings. Instead, struggle

---

54 Heidegger. *The Fundamental Question of Philosophy*

The Law of Struggle

also rules their persistence; beings are in their constancy and presence only if they are preserved and governed by struggle as their ruler...struggle is the innermost necessity of beings as a whole.

So above all it becomes clear how immediately struggle... pervasively reigns over the Being of beings as such. For struggle proves to be setting things into Being and holding them there, by making them emerge yet holding them fast... This means: the essence of Being is struggle; every Being passes through decision, victory and defeat.

A being comes into Being, in and through struggle, when it is set out. Set out — into where? Into the visibility and perceptibility of things in general; but this means into openness, unconcealment, truth.[55]

The Heraclitean worldview was institutionalized in the Nazi *Reich* thanks to the work of Alfred Bäumler, who advised Nazi leader Alfred Rosenberg, Minister and "Representative for the Supervision of the Ideological and Intellectual Education of the NSDAP". Ashley Woodward, an expert in Nietzschean philosophy, points to the ideas of Bäumler as the official interpretation of Nazi Heracliteanism.

Bäumler's interpretation in *Nietzsche: Philosopher and Politician* was recognized as the official Nazi interpretation. The concept of will is presented as Heraclitean: moving forces, becoming. Bäumler emphasizes the Nietzschean notion of power, understanding the *Will to Power* as forces in constant struggle. Bäumler rejects any interpretation of Hegelian synthesis, because it would imply the triumph of one side. Bäumler rejects any stable being, arguing that the *Will to Power* implies constant conflict without stability. For Bäumler, all knowledge, morals and cultural values are expressions of power.[56]

---

55 Heidegger. *On the Essence of Truth*
56 Ashley Woodward. *Understanding Nietzscheanism*

National Socialism - Its Principles and Philosophy

Alfred Bäumler was perhaps the most influential Nazi philosopher. It was he who gave depth to the National Socialist concept of "life as a struggle". An early member of the NSDAP, he was National Director (*Reichsamtsleiter*) of the Department of Science of the so-called "Rosenberg Office" (*Amt Rosenberg*), responsible for the cultural leadership of the *Reich*. Bäumler was the thinker most determined to link Nietzsche with National Socialism and to assimilate the pre-Socratic appraisal of *Polemos* as the essence of existence. As an admirer of the Heroic Age of the Greeks and especially of the pre-metaphysical thought of Heraclitus, Alfred Bäumler fought to update this original myth and to transform it into the central axis of National Socialist thought.

> We are certain that the only value system that could save Europe from anarchy is one that can demonstrate an intrinsic similarity to the Greek system. The discovery of the Hellenic world implies nothing less than the presentation of a new era that surpasses the Gothic and the Enlightenment. For us the Hellenic is not merely a comparison of systems of value that can be compared to the Roman, the Iranian or the Hindu. We base ourselves on the correct intuition, expressed by Winckelmann, Hölderlin and Nietzsche, that our future will be decided in our acceptance of Hellas. From Nietzsche onwards the Germanic and the Hellenic are face to face on equal terms.[57]

This re-appraisal of Hellenic antiquity is now confused with a kind of Nazi neoclassicism, but what mattered to National Socialism was not to copy an artistic style but to sink into the depths of Greek thought to synthesize it into a new Western culture.

> The Greek style is not a reproduction of the Greek way of life, of its landscapes and its inhabitants, no; it is a proclamation of the essential Greek body and spirit. It is not the diffusion of a particular work, a theme or an artist, but diffusion of the Greek world itself, which brings us face to face with Hellenism.[58]

---

57 Alfred Bäumler. *Hellas and Germania*
58 Hitler. *Cultural Speech in Nuremberg September 6, 1938*

The Law of Struggle

For Hitler, the Greek cultural heritage was equal to Germanic culture since both were heiresses of the Indo-European tradition. But facing uncertainty due to the lack of archaeological evidence of the true primitive inhabitants of the Germanic sphere, Hitler preferred to associate himself with the Greek tradition, which he considered safer ground from which to base the new Nazi culture.

> Somewhere a skull is found and the whole world says, "This is what our ancestors looked like!" Who knows whether Neanderthal man was not really still an ape! Clearly our ancestors do not come from those times! Our country may have only consisted of mud and they may have simply crossed it. If somebody asks for our ancestors we should always to refer to the Greeks.[59]

For Hitler, after the collapse of Greco-Roman culture, it was necessary to wait until the Renaissance, the cultural period preferred by the *Führer*, to see a valuable culture again. Hitler was therefore a Hellenist more than a Germanist, one reason why he was so cautious about the uncertain past of the Germanic tribes, as why he was not much excited by the medieval cultural legacy or gothic obscurity, although the paganism of the Germanic tribes and the chivalrous sagas did cloud the romantic minds of many Nazis.

For the Hitlerist Worldview, the Heraclitean idea was the foundation of a new post-Western cultural epoch. For Nazi thinkers, the Western world had to be overcome because it was based on Platonic idealism, a cultural construction that denied nature. For Bäumler the real world was a world of perpetual conflict and the new man, that *Übermenschen* that National Socialism intended to create, must be a man who bravely looked at his earthly essence.

> Europe has been under pressure for centuries, it is as if from the Middle Ages something has been sought and cannot be found. A way of life, a lost unity, an essential security of being human. Historically, Nietzsche represents the end of the Middle Ages.

---
[59] Hitler. *Table Talk*

His philosophy is an image of the Heraclitean world. This is a world that is never reassured, where becoming is always present. Becoming means struggle and victory. Heraclitus of Ephesus said: "Conflict is the Father of all things", he was the thinker to whom Nietzsche was connected from the beginning. The world and people are Heraclitally seen in the way they really are: emerged from the unknown creative depths, an eternal law of justice, of struggle, where the form maintains or sinks. This way of seeing the world is called "Heroic Realism". Nietzsche is the great philosopher of realism. Restoring the real world is the task.

Nietzsche fought against Eleatism, whose greater promoter was Plato. Of the ancient Hellenes Plato is the one who, for lack of courage, does not see the "value of reality". "Plato is afraid of facing reality, so he flees to the Ideal", says Nietzsche in "The Twilight of the Idols". Since Platonic philosophy adapts to a lack of historical sense, to a lack of representation of becoming, it looks all rigid, suspicious, mummified. This is an Egyptism. Plato has strayed from the Hellenic instinctive foundation and has been influenced by Orientalism by giving to philosophy an idolatrous meaning, a variety of priestly power. Nietzsche said: "I take with great reverence the name of Heraclitus at my side". Senses do not lie; denounce the lie of substance, unity, duration, even reason. Senses show us the becoming, what happens, the change, this is the truth. Heraclitus is right in saying that the world of appearances is the only one. Nietzsche takes sides with the senses and his supposed error of perception against the truth of reason.

For Nietzsche, the truth of the idealists is precisely the error. Through our senses we have access to the world itself since our body knows things as they are in themselves, because it is itself a thing. Nietzsche's philosophy is anti-Christian, anti-Platonic and anti-idealist. For Nietzsche, the Platonic idealist places evasion before reality. For Nietzsche the senses and the body are the only organs of knowledge. Man is the testimony that tremendous forces can be set in motion in a small creature. Whoever reaches the highest tension of the Will, whoever has greater power, also has greater justice and is closer to the truth. For justice is given in Power.[60]

STRIFE AS CULTURAL FOUNDATION

From its very beginning, the eternal law that the world was conflict and strife was an integral part of the National Socialist Worldview. And it was Hitler himself who put it in the foreground of the philosophy of Nazi life. Without the *Führer's* impulse the National Socialist Worldview would not have had Struggle as the first law of existence. Richard Weikart in his book *Hitler's Ethic* gives the concept of Struggle a paramount importance in Hitler ethics:

> The eternal *Law of Struggle*, in Hitler's view, produced all that was good in the world. It must continue, if further progress were to be made. Trying to escape the *Law of Struggle* would only… contribute to decline and degeneration.

In *Mein Kampf* Hitler stated that humans could not escape the 'iron logic of Nature,' since "his action against Nature must lead to his own doom.' Several pages later he commented, 'Those who want to live, let them fight, and those who do not want to fight in this world of eternal struggle do not deserve to live. Even if this were hard—that is how it is!' Using the term struggle in… his speeches and writings, Hitler often portrayed it as a universal law of nature, from which there is no escape. He regularly quoted the famous statement by the Greek philosopher Heraclitus that struggle is the father of all things. He frequently referred to the *Law of Struggle*, the eternal and inescapable struggle.

In a speech to military officers, [Hitler said] 'struggle and thus war is the father of all things. Whoever casts even a glance at nature as it is, will find this principle confirmed as valid for all organisms and for all

---

60   Alfred Bäumler. *Nietzsche, Philosopher and Politician*

happenings not only on this earth, but even far beyond it. The entire universe appears to be ruled only by this one idea.

Otto Dietrich later recalled that Hitler perpetually talked about struggle. Hitler based his morality on the laws of nature. One of Hitler's secretaries, Traudl Junge, confirms Dietrich's conclusions. 'His religion was the laws of nature.' She then explained that the law of nature Hitler invoked most often was the *Law of Struggle*, which humans could never escape, because we are 'children of nature.'

Weikart continues with a long series of quotations where Hitler speaks about eternal struggle as the great law of nature and foundation of the true Being of man and the universe. According to Weikart, Hitler was anti-idealist and anti-Platonic. For Max Domarus, the compiler of Hitler's speeches, existence as a struggle was the standard theme of the *Führer's* proclamations. And, truly, a review of these texts reveals hundreds of references to the law of eternal conflict. For Hitler, struggle was a law of nature and, therefore, a divine law.

> We must test Him as the creator of the world according to His *Law of Struggle* for existence.[61]

There is no doubt that for Hitler the laws of nature were good, emanating from the creative principle of the universe, laws that tended to a positive result that did not have to be avoided.

> The struggle is continuous. All life will never be anything more than struggle. We are born for the fight.[62]

In the manuals for leaders of the SS, the struggle was highlighted as the first law of the NS Worldview and only from this law was the entire National Socialist policy built.

> Struggle is the foundation of nature. When we look at the world

---

61 Hitler. *Speeches and Proclamations 1932-45*
62 Hitler. Discourse 1933, in *Speeches and Proclamations 1932-45*

The Law of Struggle

with open eyes, we see a cruel struggle of domination, a struggle for being or non-being. All must fight for existence, for food, for the soil. Plants seek to displace others by mastery of their living space, animals fight against animals.[63]

For National Socialism, courage and overcoming were born from struggle.

We see Struggle as an irrefutable law of life, because only in the eternal struggle is the condition of all selection, of all elite and vigorous people. Only from Struggle can the great be born. Struggle formed Germanic man. Struggle accompanies all his essence. Fight with yourself, fight with fate, fight with the hostile environment. In fierce battles, he dominates destiny and fights for his people, united to nature and, therefore, with a divine way of life. Struggle is the divine law to educate and be educated.[64]

For Jay Hatheway in his study *In Perfect Formation: SS Ideology and the SS-Junkerschule-Tolz*, Nazi ideology was based especially on the concern for the conflictive aspect of becoming, life as eternal struggle.

Notes from the extensive instructor's records reveal concern for the struggle, the dynamics of a world in conflict.[65]

The formational schools and the "Education Office of the SS" started from the premise that life was a constant struggle. Edwige Thibaut, a scholar and editor of the *Guidance Notebooks* (*Leitheft*), the most important publication of ideological formation for SS officers, agrees with the fundamental aspect of conflict in the SS worldview.

In his address to the chiefs of instruction of July 44, Himmler defined the purpose of the notebooks for officers. Each chapter

---

63 SS-Hauptamt. *SS-Man and Blood Questions*
64 SS-Hauptamt. *Notebooks for the Teaching of the Worldview*
65 Jay Hatheway. *In Perfect Formation*

must bring out the notions of perpetual combat on this earth; there is never peace only struggle.[66]

The prism of a universe in eternal conflict was so important to the SS that it set itself the task of finding a scientific basis to prove this principle as a universal order. At the time when the Renaissance vision of the universe still dominated scientific culture, the SS sponsored the astronomical theory of Hans Hörbiger, an engineer and space researcher who developed a revolutionary theory of the universe. In 1936, the SS signed a protocol with Alfred Hörbiger, son and heir of the astronomer (who had died in 1931), in which it pledged financial support for research under the Hörbigerian theoretical paradigm.

Hörbiger's research, developed at the end of the 19th century and published in 1913 in the book *The Glacial Cosmogony of Hörbiger. A New History of the Development of the Universe and the Solar System*, gave a new theory about the origin of the universe. Instead of an elegant universe (*cosmos*), as hitherto all scientific theories proposed, Hörbiger spoke of a universe in conflict, becoming and expanding. The theory of a universe in perpetual struggle, instead of theories that spoke of a heavenly order, of the music of the spheres, and of the perfection of the stars, was what the SS sought to lay the foundations of the laws of its Worldview. Conflict as essence and origin, not only of the organisms of the earth but of the very universe, gave support and validity to the Worldview. The Hörbigerian theory was classified by Hitler as one of the most important in history, a revolution of thought and a true cosmogony.

> I shall construct... an observatory in which will be represented the three great cosmological conceptions of history—those of Ptolemy, of Copernicus and of Hörbiger.[67]

Bernard Mees, in his study *The Science of the Swastika*, reports that National Socialism was assertive in boosting the value of Hörbiger,

---
66   Edwige Thibaut. *The SS Order*
67   Hitler. *Table Talk*

who had the vision to advance theories that explained many enigmas of astrophysics in the stage prior to the invention of radio telescopes and the Big Bang theory.

WARRIOR ETHICS

The law of life as a struggle was not thought of by National Socialism as a vindication of violence and aggression or as a feeling of constant hostility and aggression. For Eduard Paul Tratz, SS biologist and Major (SS-*Sturmbannführer*), life as a struggle was understood as a natural law, which even in the tenderest newborn immersed in the most apparent tranquility and peace, acted silently in corporeality and in the different biological systems.

> Every living being must constantly strive for its existence, whether it is a plant, an animal, or a man. Natural struggle extends to all phases of life. The first moment of the life of a creature is already a form of struggle for air and food. But there will be still all sorts of struggles, fighting against the environment, against the elements, the heat and the cold, the dryness and the humidity, the shadow, the light. To this is added the struggle for a sexual partner, for reproduction, for a son, living space and finally against the personal enemy. In the body of each living being, whether a single-celled amoeba or a multicellular plant, an animal or a man, an assimilation of air, soil or food is constantly being carried out, this is stored as an energy. In addition, each living being is subject to a process of constant evolution and thus the community is continuously transformed. Preserving needs a perpetual struggle. Life is rooted in the struggle. A life without struggle is absolutely unthinkable.[68]

For Nazism, life as a struggle was not synonymous with war, even though war was a form of struggle. For the Nazis the struggle was synonymous with overcoming the barriers that prevented adaptation and preservation,

---

68   Dr. Eduard Paul Tratz. Struggle in Nature. *Guidance Notebooks*, SS-Hauptamt

so instead of bringing destruction this law was aimed at giving life. For National Socialism, a man who was conscious of life as a struggle had to promote the increase of will and resistance in the performance of his work, and when he was faced with physical fight or war, his motivation should be framed in promoting natural and vital values.

> We find the struggle in every aspect of life and nature. The struggle leads to a natural order. The struggle produces a constant selection. Man cannot be subtracted from this eternal *Law of Struggle*. Already, birth is a mother's victory in the fight for the existence of humanity. In his life, man fights daily for his existence. Biologically it is the severity of the environment that makes combative life possible. Accepting the struggle means the prerequisite for building character. The struggle is an expression of an attitude and therefore a spiritual fact. When a person fights for ignoble reasons he destroys the culture and sins against the *Law of Struggle*. The struggle for genuine ideals creates a community of heroes. The personality of a firm character does not join the struggle without giving him a genuine affirmation of life. These are the models of the mature generation. Its spirit encourages the artist to create. Work is also a form of struggle. The peasant always lives according to the *Law of Struggle*. All life in nature and in man reflects this law of life. Without struggle there is no freedom, without struggle there is no life. The one who wants to live must fight. But the awareness that all kinds of work is under the *Law of Struggle* was lost. One only sees the *Law of Struggle* in war, although there it only displays its destructive aspect. Only through National Socialism have we found a way to affirm *the Law of Struggle* at work as well as in all areas of life.[69]

For Hitler, the *Law of Struggle* was not necessarily synonymous with destruction or death. Success in the struggle for existence also meant for the *Führer* the preservation of life.

---

69 NS Leadership Staff of the High Command of the Armed Forces. *Struggle as Life Law*

The Law of Struggle

Politics is history in the making. History itself represents the progression of a people's struggle for survival. I use the phrase "struggle for survival" intentionally here, because in reality every struggle for daily bread, whether in war or peace, is a never-ending battle against thousands and thousands of obstacles, just as life itself is a never-ending battle against death. Human beings know no more than any other creature in the world why they live, but life is filled with the longing to preserve it... While the satisfaction of the eternal hunger guarantees self-preservation, the gratification of love secures its furtherance. In truth, these two impulses are the rulers of life. And even if the fleshless esthete protests against such a claim a thousand times, the fact of his existence already refutes his protest. Whatever is made of flesh and blood can never escape the laws that condition its development... a policy that is fundamentally peaceful will be just as damaging and disastrous as a policy that only knows war as the single weapon... Because one does not make policies in order to be able to die; rather, one may only sometimes allow men to die in order that the people can live. The goal is the preservation of life and not heroic death or, least of all, cowardly resignation.[70]

For National Socialism, this warrior ethic was possible to the extent that the *Law of Struggle* was assimilated differently by man in comparison with other organisms on earth. In the most basic organisms it took on a ruthless aspect. In the animal world, the struggle was not appeased by any consideration, but in man the struggle did not take on such a drastic aspect, not even in war. For National Socialism the examples of the animal and plant kingdom were examples of how the organisms of the earth were led by the hegemony of the *Law of Struggle* but in no case should be presented as examples to imitate. For the Nazi Worldview, the human warrior ethic had drawn certain limits that differentiated it from animal instinct. However, this ethical separation did not mean for National Socialism some kind of ontological difference between human beings and other living beings, but only a different approach to fulfilling an unavoidable law of life.

---

70 Hitler. *Second Book*

Hostility exists in the animal kingdom among the great as well as the small. Danger haunts every living being. Even the orderly bees and the laborious and peaceful ants have their militias. But if for man's struggles: for bread, for position in the community and between peoples, examples from the animal world are used, something must be clarified: animals fight instinctually, in the animal world there are no ethical considerations. In human beings, however, there is a well developed ethic of struggle, for example, not attacking the helpless or in developing a just social order. This proves the difference between the struggle for life of man and that of the animal world. However, examples of the animal and plant world are presented because they clearly illustrate the eternal struggle in its most extreme forms, the war of all against all. But this difference of warrior morality between humans, plants and animals, does not mean a biological barrier. A division between an organic world and a world of the eternal spirit is emphatically rejected. Therefore we take charge of the eternal order of nature but not in a silly way, or arbitrarily, as it might seem at first glance, but with the goal of a natural order in itself.[71]

STRUGGLE AS DIVINE ORDER

For Nazism, a universe in conflict and the denial of another reality different from this immanent plane of eternal struggle did not mean some kind of atheism or cold mechanism. For National Socialism the *Life-Laws* left the door open to the belief in a creator, although, this time sharing the essence of struggle and conflict with their creatures. The doctor in Nietzschean philosophy and official of the SS Education Office, SS Major (*SS-Sturmbannführer*) Gerhart Schinke, through his writings in the *Guidance Notebooks*, emphasized the necessity of framing the *Law of Struggle* in this anti-dualist view of the universe.

As the *Führer* has said, National Socialism teaches in a luminous way the reality of the most precise scientific knowledge and

---

71 NS Leadership Staff of the High Command of the Armed Forces. *Struggle as Life Law*

expresses it clearly. Our piety bows unconditionally to the greatness of the divine *Life-Laws*. We have but one prayer: Duly to carry out the duties that derive from it. National Socialism deduces its truth from the observation of the world. It is a true philosophy. The strong man accepts the world as it is. The world is a place of beauty and at the same time an immense battlefield of eternal combat, but this will not cause the heart of a German to believe that the earth is a valley of tears. The separation of God and the world comes from a foreign way of thinking. Procreation and birth are not sins nor guilt, but fulfillment of the divine will. Death is not the consequence of sin, but a law of life. Need and destiny.

The *Führer* once said: in our program we find no mysterious intuition, but a lucid knowledge. There were times when obscurity was a necessary condition for the efficacy of certain doctrines; today we live in a time when light is the foundation of the success of our affairs. The light of science illuminates the eternal truths of National Socialist ideology. It is the outcome of the struggle of science, as well as the affirmation of our nature. Fighting for knowledge and for light and truth has always been regarded by the obscurantist world as heresy.

Today we again know that the law of the world is also that of our lives as men, just as the earth remains in the orbit of the sun, we men must remain faithful to the *Life-Laws*. To deny the divine character of nature is to despise the world and life on earth. The man who only represents God in the afterlife does not know the true respect for his own person, nor respect for what grows and blooms on the earth. We see paradise in the beauty of the earth a thousand times blessed and sacred. Here Rosenberg's phrase applies: if one considers our veneration of the earth as impious and atheist, one would also have to consider the existence of a creator and his laws as sacrilegious. Every organism fights for its life and the world becomes an image of perpetual struggle, battle is the means used by nature to maintain vigorous life, to guarantee to the world its Great Health.[72]

This belief in an immanent divinity, of nature and her laws, was reflected in the so-called "Belief in God" (*Gottgläubig*), a naturalistic faith, without deities or dogmas, which considered the world and its laws as part of a divine order. The "Belief in the Divinity" did not have any formal organization but was restricted to individual consciousness. Most members of the SS declared themselves "believers of the divinity" before identifying themselves as Christians, atheists or pagans.

For Anton Holzner, a literary pseudonym of the SS Major (SS-*Sturmbannführer*) Albert Hartl, an ideologist through his role as an expert on the religious enemies of the NS-Worldview, the divine order was eternal conflict and the new man had to be the echo of that natural order. Conflict was then shaped as the axis of value around which a whole new Nazi ethic would turn. For Hartl, God or Providence shared the same essence as the universe. The divinity therefore was immanent, his body was nature. Combat was revealed as a divine order and the struggle for preservation was presented as a mandate of Providence. This belief rejected religious formalisms, the objectification of divinities and, above all, human fragmentation in different essences. He also understood the divine substance as movement and struggle, and thought of transcendence as a projection of life in the offspring.

> For the Nordic man, body, soul and spirit form an inseparable unity. The Nordic man believes in eternal life, in his children and grandchildren, in his acts and the work for which he lives. Further on, he believes in continuing to live according to the eternal forces of the divine, in whatever form. For the Germanic man, life is the same as movement. If you are threatened with staying calm then there is something wrong with your body. The history of the Germanic people is a constant movement, a constant conflict. Being a person in movement means being open to the course of life and the evolutionary laws of this world. One of life's greatest experiences is constant development,

---

72   Gerhart Schinke. The eternal *Life Laws. Guidance Notebooks*, SS-Hauptamt

changing over and over again. This is the call of God, the call to be in movement. People on the move do not rest and do not find peace. The Germanic man believes in a superior and divine energy but are distanced from magic. Other people who bear the heavy burden of magical forces, the mysticism of amulets, secret meanings, numerology or magic words, and the effect of foreign ceremonies.[73]

SS Brigadier (*SS-Oberführer*) Kurt Ellersiek, one of the most important developers of the NS-Worldview through his work as ideological educator of the university-educated elites of the SS, was another who defended the law of conflict as part of the divine order.

> Life means fighting, we face this principle inexorably and with hardness. Either that order is accepted in the best possible way or abandoned and we die. To live means to fight, this order that Providence has given distinguishes the master from the slave. There have always been times when it has been thought possible to circumvent this mandate, in which it was believed that struggle was an abomination, in which it was a question of transferring the struggle of this world to another. But now we are in this age of accumulated energies, with a combative and creative spirit and an unusual will to live. We approve of life because we love the fight; we approve the fight because we love life. For us life is a battlefield that Providence has given us, a providential order.[74]

This vision of a world in conflict, as a divine order and cause of life, made it impossible for the world to be thought of as a "valley of tears", as is often the case in transcendental religions. For Nazism, the *Law of Struggle* was an order inherent to the universe, an order that created infinite possibilities to develop life and inventiveness. It was there that Hitler found the spaces that gave meaning to life.

---

73 Anton Holzner, pseudonym of Albert Hartl. *Master Life*
74 Kurt Ellersieck. *Our Life,* in *House of the SS Troop, SS-Hauptamt*

All life is paid for with blood. If a man doesn't like this notion of life, I advise him to renounce life altogether—for it proves he is not suited for the struggle. In any case, on the margin of this continual struggle, there's so much pleasure in living. So why be sad at what is so, and could not be otherwise! The creative forces make their home in the bosom of the optimist.[75]

THE WAY OF HEROIC REALISM

The world in conflict: pain, but also the joyful possibility of development and improvement was the theme of the Nazi poet, SS officer Kurt Eggers. Eggers became a kind of Ernst Jünger of World War II, a popular writer who navigated among the transfiguring mysteries of the conflict. Eggers was very realistic in describing the war's negative aspect, its destruction and death, but at the same time described the positive aspect of the conflict, the birth of new possibilities and the transfiguration of man into a heroic realist. Eggers wrote of the renewing force of struggle through his editorial work for the SS newspaper *Das Schwarze Korps* and then as an active correspondent and warrior on the eastern front. His heroic death in the Russian theater was recognized by *Reich* leaders who named a detachment in his honor, *SS-Standarte Kurt Eggers*.

> Nature destroys the human being who does not know how to protect himself. Is it therefore cruel? Rain sometimes becomes bothersome for us, it makes staying in the open almost unbearable. Is it therefore the scourge of mankind? Or the frost? Or the storm? ...Ignoring this would be a sign of incapacity to live! Nature is neither good nor evil... The force governing it—the Law—makes grow and perish, germinate and mature, and the eternal rhythm of the universe has no ear for complaints and groans. The human being must confront nature, come to terms with it. If necessary, take up the struggle with it, at best, fathom its secrets and make its many expressions useful to himself.

---

75 Hitler. *Table Talk*

The Law of Struggle

Man has snatched away from nature countless secrets and made them useful to himself, his progress, his security. Yes, many an allegedly hostile and destructive force, after the recognition of its law, became man's ally... The world as nature's form of manifestation is an eternal alternation of life and decline, and therefore of attack, perseverance, succumbing and becoming anew.

The world is neither good nor evil. It is a great battlefield, a site of eternal struggle, of everlasting conflict. And we must enter into this eternal war of the world, we bearers of life. Not because we created this war, rather the world simply does not show itself to us differently. We also cannot change the essence of a force of nature.

We thank creative nature that gave us the capacity for hostility. Through it, we are able to develop energies which are constructive and formative, organizing and law-giving... The reality of this world is filled with fighting and conflict, struggle for assertion. And this reality cannot be hidden away by any doctrine, by any theory, by any ideology, by any ever so happy message. Strong, warlike human beings, who have not lost their instinct... see in the struggle of the world the great opportunity for the development of their nature... Our *Führer* once spoke the clear and distinct words "National Socialism is a coolly realistic doctrine of the sharpest scientific character". We National Socialists know that these words are an affirmation of the reality of this life and this world, which cannot ever be evaded. Whoever wants to live, must fight; There is simply no non-combative life. At least not a healthy, creative and thus blessed life!...Again and again, excuses are on hand, nothing is easier for us than to veil the truth. We only need to close our eyes in order not to see it. The *Führer* first created in National Socialism the cold doctrine of reality, which, sublime above fear and pain, depicted the world as it is. So we soldiers gained more than a Worldview; we learned to see through the world.[76]

---

[76] Kurt Eggers. *Hostility*

National Socialism - Its Principles and Philosophy

For Eggers, the revelation of life as struggle required an act of great inner honesty to free himself from all the culturally inculcated idealistic worldviews. For Eggers, the only force in the world capable of revealing the reality of the *Life-Laws*, even to those most blinded by abstract ideologies, was war. In war, the eternal struggle of the universe was cruelly but relentlessly revealed. In war the mechanisms of selection, leadership, maximum effort, sacrifice and solidarity between peers were the key to success and survival. In war, selfishness, mercantilism, ideologies and theories were worthless. War was the relentless school of the *Life-Laws*. This was the path that transformed Hitler from an idealist artist into an implacable realist. Eggers, especially in his book of meditations on war, "Father of All Things," described this path of transformation. Eggers was popular because he did not speak from theory but from the battlefield, as a veteran, as a transfigured heroic realist.

> [The warrior] sees the world with the eyes of incorruptibility and recognizes, beyond the petty moods of bourgeois daily life, the moving forces of the world. So, the aware soldier loses through war, the simple and questioning attitude of the boy and becomes tough, directed to the distance with his war experience the fancifully questioning gaze of the boy and gets that hard, far-sighted, seeking gaze that seems hostile and cold to the bourgeois man. Constant exertion, having-to-overcome-oneself again and again, makes the lips narrow, and and the sight of distress and suffering, the experience of honor, dig sharp features into the the face, which thereby becomes more squared—unsoldierly people like to call it uglier... War educates through the knowledge of reality....In war, machines do not replace man. Machine guns and Panzers need men to manipulate them and crews to drive them. In war, soldiers elevate themselves out of anonymity and grow to the might of a group of passionate personalities focused on annihilation or victory.

> A generation which has passed through war... has been reeducated and can never again return to that state from which it once departed... War simply demands the mobilization of

all assets with a view toward their total employment for the achievement of the goal... The warrior gains from the experience of reality a picture of the world that leads him to a Worldview.[77]

---

[77] Kurt Eggers. *Father of All Things*

The Law of Selection

Alongside the *Law of Struggle* the National Socialist Worldview granted a place of honor to the *Law of Selection* (*Gesetz der Auslese*).

> The first law that governs the world is the *Law of Selection*: the strongest and healthiest are granted by nature the right to life. And it is right that it should be so.[78]

For Hitler "Struggle always means strength overcomes weakness" and this condition implied the *Law of Selection*.

For National Socialism, the *Law of Selection* was the method by which nature tended to specialize and improve each generation by privileging the transfer of certain characteristics to future generations and putting an end to the more useless traits in the struggle for existence. The *Law of Selection* was understood as a way to acquire evolutionary weapons in order to face life as a struggle.

> We know of the evolution of life through the fossil record. Research always shows the same thing. Older layers show the remains of simply designed organisms. The later layers show more evolution and the recent layers show the remains of the most evolved organisms. Evolution means development, change, growth, reproduction, expansion, etc. Each evolution requires large spaces of time that know no peace. The life of an individual disappears completely in the evolution of a species. With open eyes we see that in nature there is struggle without end. Battle is the law of nature. The deeper meaning of this law is that the weak perish; only the strongest survives. The goal is therefore a selection towards improvement. In National

---

78 Hitler. Construction Workers Speech. Berchtesgaden, 1937

Socialist terms this means that the common good comes before any individual good, the individual is nothing compared to the whole.[79]

But for Nazism, these criteria of natural selection had been lost as a result of Western abstractions, ideologies, and theories that had rather tended to develop strong counter-selective processes.

> Civilization has forgotten these laws of nature. Perhaps man can postpone these effects, but he will never eliminate them. Just as some species have become extinct, peoples can also disappear. Only selection maintains a race at its peak, gradually eliminating heritable traits by not allowing their wide representation in the next generation.[80]

Selection was for National Socialism, the great architect of the evolutionary paths that allowed the species to triumph in the struggle for existence and for that reason it was to lead a political, cultural and social effort to re-evaluate this principle. It was thought that selection could combat cultural decadence and the crisis leadership. For Hitler and National Socialism, the *Law of Selection* implied cultural progress through evolutionary improvement and the subsequent emergence of personalities of superior inventiveness. For Hitler, creative geniuses were not the result of education or social privilege but the product of this law of life.

> Nature has endowed creatures with unlimited fecundity, yet it has not provided the necessary food, which must be procured only with great effort. This is good and necessary, since it is the struggle for existence that produces the selection of the best. I have no doubt that great personalities arise from this method of selection.[81]

---

79 SS-Hauptamt. *SS-Man and Blood Questions*
80 SS-Hauptamt. *SS-Man and Blood Questions*
81 Hitler. *Mein Kampf*

The Law of Selection

During the National Socialist *Reich* the *Law of Selection* guided promotion through the hierarchies of the Movement and thus access to the inner circles of the State.

> The aim of any natural selection is to ensure the survival of the species. In the struggle for existence the most efficient and fertile are selected to maintain and continue life. Selection also produces an improvement in human evolution. The SS Order is responsible for ensuring that not only are the laws of natural selection respected by our people, but also that conscious and premeditated selection is made.[82]

For Nazism, selection had a biological and not a materialistic meaning, so it explicitly ruled out the utilitarian economic application of individual struggle, as in the case of liberalism. For Nazism the *Law of Selection*, if it was to have a biological basis, should aim at preservation and community vigor and not individual benefit or welfare.

> We must never extend the concept of struggle for existence to economic life, for we understand this concept biologically.[83]

The selection law determined the Nazi *Reich's* course of racial policy. All the efforts to revitalize the genetic component of the German and European people passed by way of the tough selection criteria which the Nordic race had to observe in its gestation stage.

The Biological Sense of Selection

According to the current scientific consensus there are four causes of evolutionary change. "Selection", "DNA replication error or mutation", "genetic drift" and "gene flow". Gene flow is the exchange of heritable characteristics among populations with different selection criteria. Genetic drift is the random fluctuation in the proportion

---

82 SS-Hauptamt. *NS-Dictionary*
83 SS-Hauptamt. *SS Mate Selection and Race*

of certain traits in the gene pool of a population. Replication error refers to mutations produced in genes at the time of cell reproduction. These three causes of genetic change do not have higher objectives of evolutionary specialization, nor do they tend toward adaptation or the creation of value. But, out of all these types of changes in a population's gene pool, National Socialism took only selection as an agent of evolutionary improvement. For Nazism it was through selection that all these changes could be evaluated according to their value in the struggle for existence.

During cellular reproduction, the process of copying genetic information for transfer sometimes presents certain anomalies or copy errors, which results in so-called genetic mutations. For Nazism these new heritable traits eventually came as a comparative advantage in the struggle for existence. A small mutation could produce a tiny protein variation, which resulted, for example, in a thinner lens, eventually resulting in a lighter eye color. This eye color was advantageous in the north euro-asian climate, giving a comparative advantage to its bearer. With time and as a product of selection, another eye color was discarded in those populations. The *Law of Selection* was vindicated by choosing precisely these random errors, along with proven traits, to be transferred. For the Worldview everything that did not mean comparative advantage was discarded by nature. The *Law of Selection* was the sieve by which each generation left behind inappropriate sediment when facing the struggle for existence.

For National Socialism the perpetual struggle for existence needed a plastic physiology, always adapting to new conditions and the demands of the environment. In Nazi ethics, preservation did not mean mere maintenance or stagnation, but quite the contrary. The success of preservation lay in constant change and continuous adaptation.

> Nature concentrates her attention not on the preservation of what already exists, but on the selective breeding of offspring in order to carry on the species.[84]

---

84 Hitler. *Mein Kampf*

The Law of Selection

Through the selection of advantageous heritable characteristics, groups of organisms evolved in each generation by becoming more specific, always amending their genetic heritage and looking for methods to adapt to the environment.

For the NS Worldview, just as the environment is constantly changing and moving, the generations of different groups and species were always different, privileging the transfer of only part of the total heritable characteristics and discarding the less useful parts in the struggle for preservation. The *Law of Selection* acted in nature mainly under the law of reproductive rights. In nature, reproduction was not a universal right, but a selective right. For that reason, species had to overcome terrible trials, often in brutal combat with the former holder of territorial and reproductive rights. This natural law was assimilated by National Socialism and became the basis of its policy of "correct mate selection" (*Gattenwahl*). "*The right to live is not the same as the right to give life*"[85]. With the policy of correct mate selection, National Socialism meant for the population to instinctively exercise a principle of reproductive selection that would lead to the progressive elimination of those characteristics less advantageous in the struggle for existence.

For National Socialism, so-called racial inequality was born from the *Law of Selection*, since selection guided the particular development of species and groups of organisms. These groups of organisms, being isolated and involved in selective processes oriented towards different evolutionary objectives, were genetically distanced from each other. With selection came difference, the evolutionary paths of specialization. Selection was the mechanism by which species, races and even organs emerged. That is why so-called Nazi racism sought the preservation of selection criteria and not the preservation of fixed genetic characteristics. The political mission of National Socialism was to restore the harsh selective criteria that allowed the emergence of the white race. For the Nazi Worldview the objective of the Racial Policy was not to preserve and mummify a specific anthropological type, the blue-eyed blond, nor to seek an ever elusive racial purity.

---

85 Alfred Rosenberg. *Struggle for our Worldview*

Races were for National Socialism a derivative of selection. The ultimate objective of Nazism was to preserve the selection criteria that ensured a future population would be able to withstand the arduous struggle for the existence of the ancient and successful white race, criteria that according to Hitler had taken hundreds of thousands of years to shape evolutionary successfully types.

> There are certain truths which are so obvious that the general run of people disregard them. People are so blind to some of the simplest facts in everyday life that they are highly surprised when somebody calls attention to what everybody ought to know... Walking in the garden of Nature, most men have the self-conceit to think that they know everything, yet almost all are blind to one of the outstanding principles that Nature employs in her work. This principle may be called the inner isolation which characterizes each and every living species on this earth. Even a superficial glance is sufficient to show that all the innumerable forms in which the life-urge of Nature manifests itself are subject to a fundamental law — one may call it an iron law of Nature — which compels the various species to keep within the definite limits of their own life-forms when propagating and multiplying their kind.

> Such a dispensation of nature is quite logical. Every crossing of two breeds which are not of equal standing results in a product which holds an intermediate place between the levels of the two parents... For this reason, it must eventually succumb in any struggle against a higher species. Such mating contradicts the will of Nature towards a selective improvement of life in general... The stronger must dominate and not mate with the weaker, which would signify the sacrifice of its own higher nature. Only the born weakling can look upon this principle as cruel... for if such a law did not direct the process of evolution then the higher development of organic life would not be conceivable at all.

> That is why the struggle between the various species does not

arise from a feeling of mutual antipathy, but rather from hunger and love. In both cases Nature looks on calmly and is even pleased with what happens. The struggle for daily livelihood leaves behind everything that is weak, diseased or wavering; while the fight of the male to possess the female gives to the strongest the right, or at least the possibility, to propagate his kind. This struggle is a means of furthering the health and powers of resistance of the species, thus it is one of the causes underlying the process of development towards a higher grade of being. If this were otherwise the progressive progress would cease and even a retrogression might set in… because all Nature's efforts, throughout hundreds of thousands of years, to establish an evolutionarily higher stage of being would be rendered futile.[86]

Selection And Human Groups

Nazi scientists thought selection was carried out on two levels. Great evolutionary changes produced modifications that led to the formation of organs and the physiological characteristics of adaptation. This was macroevolution, a process that led to a differentiation between species. On the other hand was microevolution, a process that referred to the small changes at intra-species level, those physiological changes that in a biological evolutionary sense allowed each generation to be better than the previous one.

Selection as the cause of micro and macro-evolution was a discovery of Gerhard Heberer, biologist, anthropologist, historian and geneticist, as well as an SS Captain and member of the "SS Race and Settlement Main Office" (RuSHA). Heberer, therefore, made selection out to be the greatest evolutionary factor, not only at the macro evolutionary level but also in the day-to-day lives of groups of organisms. The selection policies advocated by the Nazi State and the SS were understood as a mechanism that would generate changes not only at the qualitative level but also at the anthropological level. Rather than regaining a lost purity, Nazi selection laws would generate new human

---

86   Hitler. *Mein Kampf*

capabilities, reflected in new and future phenotypes. Nazi scientists knew therefore that so-called racial purity was non-existent. The idea of specialization and differentiation in groups of organisms brought with it the controversial idea of the common origin of all species on earth. In this sense, the NS Worldview assumed the brotherhood of all organisms as a scientific fact that confirmed the idea of differentiation and change through selection.

> The theory of evolution, knowledge of the interrelatedness of all living beings, also offers man the opportunity to live out the attitudes and behaviors of the entire living world. The earth has not always been as it is now; it has been formed and developed, events in the cosmos giving it shape and developing countless numbers of living forms. The diversity that we see today has developed from simple forms. Each living being goes back in a long chain to its distant ancestors through reproduction and propagation. Already in the pre-scientific period man has recognized family relations in nature.[87]

For Nazism, change came out of this natural unity. Selection then created different, specialized groups through evolution. Among humans, selection had generated groups with unique heritable characteristics.

National Socialism understood that human groups derived from a common trunk, perhaps originating in Africa or Asia, but for the Nazi scientists that did not change the fact that the crystallization of the inherited Europid factors into the Europid form had occurred in the Eurasian north. For National Socialism, the selection criteria to which this human group was subjected—trapped in the northern ices during the last ice age—resulted in the specific sequence of heritable characteristics that correspond to the white race. In the same way, other isolated and specialized human groups became, in the process of their adaptation, the black and yellow races, and other races that had been lost in previous periods.

---

[87] SS-Hauptamt. *Teaching Plan for Worldview Education of the SS and Police*

The Law of Selection

Only once climatic conditions improved would the members of this small and specialized human group have begun their migrations. More than fifteen thousand years ago small groups with their roots in the Eurasian north would have dispersed throughout Europe, Asia and even America. From the Neolithic, a small white population was concentrated in the Baltic, later settling in the Caucasus, where it gave way to a successful culture, the proto Indo-European. In the Iron Age the migrations of the indefatigable Indo-Europeans — called Aryans by the Nazis — went everywhere between the Indus Valley and Europe, including the Mediterranean coast and the Middle East. They were the peoples who formed the successful cultures of the Greeks, Romans, Celts, Germanics, Persians and Indians, among several others. For Hitler, *contra* the guardians of the Germanic cultural superiority, the white race, though it had originated in the harsh conditions of the Eurasian North, had borne its greatest fruits on the shores of the Mediterranean in the time of Greco-Latin, classical culture.

For National Socialism, the original heritable characteristics of the white human group were those that are commonly associated with the Nordic type. These characteristics were born in the struggle for existence among the northern ices. It was very clear to the NS Worldview that, since the end of the Ice Age, the increasingly large white human group, as well as the other human groups, had neither the time nor the isolation needed to undergo such intense selection processes. If this were the case, isolated races, constantly adapting through selection, would have been transformed into species. Hence the ambiguity of some texts when using the terms race or species when talking about these ancestral human groups.

However, there was consensus that the evolutionary changes of the last millennia had produced minor changes. For Otto Reche, a world-renowned anthropologist and member of the NSDAP, as well as for Gerhard Heberer, tens of thousands of years ago the white race showed stable physiological characteristics. Even so, the Nazi consensus held that evolution did not stop, and that in the last millennia micro-evolutionary changes had taken place. One of them was gracilization, that is, the acquisition of more stylized and less coarse contours.

Adaptations would also have been recorded in the endocrine, nervous and other more plastic systems of physiology.

The persistence of Nordic phenotypes, believed to be confirmed by the similar features depicted in Greek and Celtic sculpture, showed that the evolutionary paths to producing a new human race took thousands of years, whenever there was selection oriented towards specialization. For Nazism phenotypic variety of the present was explained better by genetic flow, i.e. by racial mixing. Nazism therefore ruled out the existence of modern "races". Germans, Italians, Jews, etc. were peoples (*völk*), rather than races (*rasse*). Germany was thus understood as the community of a racially diverse people (*Volksgemeinschaft*) and its citizens were comrades in that community (*Volksgenossen*).

THE NORDIC RACE

The racial consensus of National Socialism understood that the nations of Europe had formed on the basis of a mixture of prehistoric races. The NS Worldview rejected the ideas of a nationalism that spoke of the exceptionality of a German race as though there were a biological difference with other European peoples. Christopher M. Hutton, an anthropologist at the University of Hong Kong, gives an account of the professional synthesis achieved by National Socialist science.

> There was near universal agreement that each *Volk* (people) was made up of elements drawn from more than one race. Thus the German Volk did not have a single racial identity; it was racially mixed, and in racial terms overlapped with the membership of other Völker (peoples). This view remained academic orthodoxy in the racial anthropology of the Third Reich.[88]

Walther Gross, director of the "Office of Racial Policy of the NSDAP" (*NS-Rassenpolitisches Amt*), was adamant on this score, as was Richard Hildebrandt, *SS-Obergruppenführer* in charge of the "SS Race and Settlement Main Office" (*SS-Rasse-und Siedlungshauptamt, RuSHA*).

---

[88] Christopher M. Hutton. *Race and the Third Reich*

> Any statement about a *German race* is factually and politically wrong, even harmful.[89]

For the NS Worldview, Nordic heritable characteristics were those of the Europid or white human group. Only through contact with other human groups had the Europids acquired their present variety of types, giving way to the subsets of the white trunk. These subsets were initially termed as sub-races, namely Fallid, Alpine, Mediterranean, Dinaric and Baltic-eastern. In this scientific consensus it was understood that, in spite of the generalized process of genetic flow in Europe, the Nordic element remained as a common substrate within the German and European people. Richard von Hoff, a renowned member of the Party, a senior official and editor of the influential biological science journal "Race", was the promoter of this idea.

> While Germans were indeed largely Mischlinge with Dinaric and Alpine blood, the Nordic race was what united all Germans.[90]

For Nazi scientists, Nordic genetic inheritance was not pure in any part of the world. For the Nazis it was not possible to find Nordic individuals, only individuals with higher or lower percentages of Nordic blood, percentages distributed across external, internal, physical and psychological hereditary characteristics.

> The strictly academic position was that it was not possible to find a 100% Nordic individual.[91]

These heritable traits were scattered across the nations and peoples of Europe and even the world. All that was needed to revitalize the Nordic race was to update the selection criteria that had already operated for millennia. These criteria would allow Nordic heritable traits to re-develop and express themselves in a new, transnational elite. The important National Socialist psychologist and SA Gerhard

---
89 Walther Gross, quoted by Hutton
90 Richard von Hoff, quoted in Hutton
91 Christopher M. Hutton. *Race and the Third Reich*

Pfahler, synthesized the objectives of racial policy and its selective orientation. Insofar as an individual had a combination of Nordic and non-Nordic genes, his importance to the community did not lay in his appearance or psychology. "Pfahler argued that the measure of an individual's worth within the *Volk* was their contribution and achievements *(Leistung)* in its service."[92].

Many have accused National Socialism of being obsessed with racial purity and eugenics. And although this occurred in some circles, for Hitler the important thing was the revival of the rigorous and relentless *Law of Selection*, not some effort to preserve living fossils. In this sense, and as instructional manuals indicated, racial theories were a derivative of the Worldview, not its essence. That is why the selection law was above the efforts of the guardians of racial purity.

For National Socialism, a community of clones or a society where the strictest artificial genetic intervention was applied would never restore the physiological vigor that would allow it to face the struggle for existence. For National Socialism, racial purity meant nothing if it was not a derivative of selective processes. Nordic physical characteristics were understood as an indicator of the possibility of value, good raw material with which to start selection processes, but not an indication of value in itself. This was confirmed when the Nazis confronted the subject of Scandinavia. Commonly thought of as a great source of genetic value, National Socialism was rather cautious in sowing hope about these populations. Contact during the war with countries like Norway disappointed some Nazis who had misinterpreted the racial doctrines of the NS Worldview. The SS, on the other hand, aware of the *Life Laws*, was not surprised, addressing the subject in several texts in which Scandinavia was cataloged as a counter-selective society, a people without historical destiny and with an ambivalent, even reactionary, attitude towards cultural awakening under the NS Worldview.

"In Germany there is a lack of clarity regarding the actual situation

---

92   Hutton

The Law of Selection

in the North. Instead, idealized conceptions often prevail, and an optimistic illusion about the victory of the Nordic idea among other peoples who are so closely related to us. These preconceived ideas, which did not coincide with reality, were disappointed. Exaggerated hopes that looked to Norway were not fulfilled. The Norwegians did not correspond with the imagined ideal. They are men with important defects, whose external appearance only partially agrees with the Nordic ideal. Even when the external image seemed to correspond to the ideal, the spiritual attitude was lacking. We had come to a country where liberalism was in full bloom, where long peace had made pacifism a basic, almost natural inclination. There were no acute problems that needed immediate solutions. It is sufficient to consider some points of the racial doctrine of National Socialism in order to draw conclusions about Norwegian relations. The *Führer* has mentioned the great importance of the diverse composition of the related races of our people and has spoken of a happy mixture. On the other hand as it is known, each race carries some characteristics that are both good and bad. Throughout history, the Nordic race has consistently demonstrated that it does not demonstrate its most valuable characteristics more than when faced with difficult conditions or rough tasks. Instead it has the foreboding characteristic of languishing in quiet periods. Not only Norway, but the whole Germanic north now lives in a period of languishing.[93]

Hitler commented sarcastically about it:

> The man of the Nordic countries is so soft that his most beautiful women pack their bags at the first opportunity to find a true man in our country.[94]

For Nazism, racial purity was not the end of their political struggles, nor even the *telos* of Racial Policy. For the NS Worldview, selective processes were what counted, even in mixed populations. These ensured survival and hardness in the struggle. For National Socialism,

---

93 H. H. Norway: *House of the SS Troop*. SS-Hauptamt
94 Hitler. *Table Talk*

the Nordic blood scattered throughout the community were the echo of the strong selective processes of antiquity, and Nazism wanted to start their project of physiological renewal by taking advantage of that potential value. For National Socialism without selection not even Nordic genes would be saved from degeneration.

Nordic Transnational

Everything indicates that the Nazi plan of racial regeneration was set up to produce strong selective processes through a culture based on the hard struggle for existence. Great demands on the youth, permanent conflict in Eastern Europe, colonization by means of high-yield productive farms, high standards at an artisanal and labor level, discipline and permanent effort in all areas, among other strict demands, were policies that sought to create a hard society and high performing people. By applying these values within a new European order Nazism wanted to renew the full potential of the Nordic heritable characteristics.

For Hutton, the policies of selection and the plan of nordification were meant to revolutionize the European political order based on the Westphalian Nation State. Nordicism would have a mandate that surpassed the narrow confines of the European nations. "The concept of a Nordic race as a transnational elite suggested a powerful racial force operating independently of modern Nation States"[95] The Nordic racial stock was thought of as a diaspora, a sort of transnational legacy, ready to be awakened through selection policies that would regenerate the languishing European populations:

> Knowledge of the importance of the *Life-Laws* has set in motion a revaluation of all things. The historical State concepts have lost their importance; dogmatic laws have weakened, compared to what is decreed by nature. Only biological laws can determine the limits of the new interconnectedness that allows us to imagine global vision of European community. The diversity of

---

95   Christopher M. Hutton. *Race and the Third Reich*

the nations of Europe is growing today into a greater common order, shifting the emphasis of national government thinking to that of the *Life-Laws* and biological processes.[96]

Working through SS lawyers like Werner Best and Reinhard Höhn, National Socialism was determined to end the concept of the State and Rule of Law (*Rechtsstaat*), concepts that underpinned the international order as well as the political theory of nationalism, the most reactionary element facing the new idea of a Nordic transnational order. Nationalism had resulted in a political movement intimately linked to a sense of belonging and identity that nourished the sovereign nation and the rule of law and order. For Nazism, German nationalism turned all identitarian sentiment over to the legal entity of the State, a social contract that allowed the existence of the nation only through a fictitious legal entity. On the contrary, for the NS Worldview the new "People's Law" would not fit in the narrow margins of the abstract legal structure of the nation state, but only within the biological element.

One of the founders of national biology jurisprudence was the *SS-Oberführer* Reihardt Höhn, director of the "State Research Institute" and law professor at the University of Berlin. Höhn promoted;

> ... the radical overcoming of the Sovereign State and its liberal tradition of the Rule of Law. The individualist state of liberalism was to be replaced by the People's Community (Volksgemeinschaft) where legal thought was directed towards the whole community.[97]

Höhn developed, and was the main exponent of, the revolutionary idea to replace the legal person of the State, transferring it from the juridical plane to the biological community entity. National Socialism, for Höhn, was to declare "war on the concept of the personality of the State". In his speech entitled *The Constitutional Position* he elaborates:

---
96 SS-Hauptamt. *Teaching Plan for Worldview Education of the SS and Police*
97 Reihardt Höhn quoted by Ingo Hueck in *Spheres of Influence and Völkisch Legal Thought..*

National Socialism - Its Principles and Philosophy

In the place of the current individualistic principle a new concept appears. The legal entity of the State is no longer the basis of constitutional law. The Community of the People is the new starting point. The juridical personality and the concept of community totally exclude one another.

SS-Obergruppenführer and Doctor of Law, Werner Best played a fundamental role in the crusade against the Nation State. Best took the concept of Great Spaces, initially promulgated in a Westphalian version by the conservative lawyer Carl Schmitt, as a basis for the expansion of National Socialism and its biologist prism. According to contemporary scholars like Christian Joerges, there was a conceptual abyss between Best's theories and conventional jurisprudence. Best sought to replace "The abstract concept of State and other interest-based formations with a people's order of Great Spaces"[98]. With Best, the controversy of the nation's foundation began between two irreconcilable sides, "biologists" and "nationalists", the latter led by Schmitt, who was gradually pushed away from circles of power.

During the war, the SS was the most enthusiastic political body in advancing the idea of a unified Europe under an order of nations based on biological identity. The spokesman for post-nationalist European unification was SS General Gottlob Berger, who designed the first pan-European army, the Waffen SS, a militia which, together with the Germanic *Reich* divisions, reached almost one million volunteers from countries across Europe, Asia, North Africa and even the Middle East.

Counter-Selection

According to Hitler, the selection processes of the Ice Age had created a unique biological type, the Europid or white human group, with Nordic characteristics. The hardness of the climate selected stronger types able to solve difficult problems in order to survive. For the racial policies of National Socialism, the key was to maintain a vigorous Europid human group. This meant maintaining the original

---

98   Quoted by Christian Joerges, *Europe a Grossraum?*

selection criteria, not worrying about maintaining a certain phenotype, characteristics that could obscure many recessive genetic anomalies.

But for National Socialism the last centuries had seen the attenuation of natural selective processes. Due to the absence of selection criteria, all the errors in genetic replication, drift alterations, and new genetic flow, certain features had been retained without going through the selective screening. When selective processes were not effective, all that effort of trial and error had no evolutionary direction and therefore lacked value in the struggle for existence. Modern man carried the heavy burden of a great number of hereditary characteristics that were totally useless and that might even threaten survival. This process was called counter-selection.

For National Socialism, counter-selection had created a weakened humanity, lacking in will and only creative when it came to inventing new methods of cultural numbing. And although modernity could provide a false sense of security, this has always presented challenges when it comes to preserving a community. Change of environment, natural disasters, epidemics, climate change, pollution, deterioration of food quality etc., were constant threats that required adaptation and ever-renewed selective processes. In the absence of harsh and primitive life, the mission of National Socialism consisted in artificially articulating these criteria through its public policies.

> "Our people have failed in their duty to survive and have contravened the natural *Law of Selection*. Nature is always organized according to divine laws. The law of natural selection reigns ruthlessly. The strong and courageous can face the thousand dangers that nature presents. Natural selection acts so that only the strong and the healthy survive and multiply by procreation. The strongest and the best fulfill their destiny in selection according to the divine laws, by maintaining of the value of the species in the eternal sense of the perpetual struggle for existence, toward its improvement and elevation. Consequently, while the *Law of Selection* reigns in nature, the nation's mismanagement has provoked a counter-selection. In

counter-selection, the "valueless" is multiplied at the expense of the valuable. The death of a people is based on this misconception of life." [99]

For Hitler, abandoning selection criteria put a people in a position of weakness, taking away the evolutionary weapons needed to confront the attacks of the environment. The German people had been weakened, replacing selection criteria with sheltered urban culture. The encounter of the *Reich's* troops with the vigorous Ukrainians during the advance into Eastern Europe, revealed to the *Führer* the harmful effect of urban counter-selective policies in Germany.

"Bormann, who has just returned from a tour of inspection of the Kolkhoz in the vicinity of General Headquarters, gave his impressions: I was much struck by the fact that in these huge open spaces one saw so many children and so few men. Such prolific breeding may one day give us a knotty problem to solve, for as a race they are much hardier by nature than we are. The men have admirable teeth, and rarely does one see a man wearing glasses. They are well fed and bursting with good health at all ages. The difficult conditions under which these men have lived for centuries have brought into being a merciless process of selection. If one of us drinks a drop of their water, he all but dies. We fill ourselves with quinine as a safeguard against malaria, while the Ukrainians are so immune, not only to malaria but to scarlet fever as well, that they can live with impunity in surroundings teeming with fleas and ticks.[100]

Walther Gross, National Leader (*Reichleiter*) of the NSDAP and Head of the "Office of Racial Policy" (*Rassenpolitisches Amt*), confirmed these ideas by pointing out through official channels that forgetting the selection criteria had been the major cause of the Germanic decline.

When people do not obey the *Life-Laws* they are on the path to disaster. Man has interfered in these matters. He has tried to

---

99 Gerhart Schinke. What do people die of? II. Selection and counter-selection, *Guidance Notebooks*, SS-Hauptamt
100 Hitler. *Table Talk*

change the laws of eternal battle and selection. These were the ancestral *Laws of Life* to which man was subject.[101]

According to psychologist and *SS-Obersturmbannfuhrer* Ludwig Eckstein, director of the "SS Education Office" (*SS-Schulungamt*), National Socialist actions ought to reverse counter-selection with artificial policies that mimicked the original selection criteria. Eckstein joined his voice to the main chorus of the National Socialist Worldview, repeated over and over again, that the National Socialist and the SS man should echo a thought rooted in the *Life Laws*, even before they think politically.

> Today the idea of selection is one of the masterpieces of the National Socialist Worldview. Human groups acquire homogenous characteristics of physical and psychic traits in the course of ten thousand years, in harmonious relation with the environment. Clear-skinned Nordic Europid mankind has been marked by the uniform and isolated Siberian Nordic Euro-Asian habitat of the Ice Age. We can easily imagine the consequences of natural selection in that space. Only those who had been subjected to the harshest conditions of existence could have survived and perpetuated themselves for the next millennia.

> To reproduce and to perpetuate was granted only to those who were ultimately revealed to be superior to that climate in that inhospitable part of the earth. Only the qualities that allowed man to vanquish nature were perpetuated and consolidated by hereditary transmission. The birth of a species is the progressive and substantial crystallization of all the qualities that make it possible to face the hardness of living conditions victoriously. The more a human group is able to master and transform the conditions of its area of life by establishing a culture faithful to the law of life, the easier it is for the individual to preserve and avoid elimination. But the laws of selection, severe in their origin, subsided and lost their vigor, finally arriving at a reverse

---

101 Walther Gross. *National Socialist Racial Policy*

process. The more a culture ages and reaches the state of late civilization, the more it loses its vigor. It even produces reverse processes. Weak and sick individuals can thus survive and reproduce, different racial types are mixed. The creative law of the species no longer seems to act upon it.

When a culture already has the characteristics of a late civilization, "selection" itself has turned into a frightful counter-selection. Conservation and evolution are slowly being questioned. The process of cultural selection sometimes arrives at an instinctive and "purely spiritual" hostility. This produces a different selection process, a cultural selection that may have a different nature than the original biological selection. The original biological meaning, that is, that men of value are favored in their reproduction, most of the time is not taken into account. National Socialism cannot conceive of its demand for selection other than with the aim of being in accordance with the biological laws at the origin of species. Leaving aside this civilizing counter-selection we see numerous attempts made to practice a conscious and methodical cultural selection. Its purpose and intention are always "to place the right man in the right place". Any conscious selection that has immediate successes that are evaluated in years and decades must be able to be carried out simultaneously through centuries, millennia and hundreds of millennia. If not, it loses all credit to the history of our species and ultimately to its divine Creator. One must therefore ensure that the idea of selection is defended and applied only to the whole of the National Socialist Worldview. All other partial and rational applications produce the opposite effect. So far, the SS has been its most appropriate instrument. The laws of the Order and its institutions are animated by the spirit of biological duty that emanates from the sense of duty towards the race, and from submission to the Creator and for that reason it has been misunderstood and misinterpreted by those who do not think in a biological way.[102]

---

102 Ludwig Eckstein. The biological meaning of selection. *Guidance Notebooks,*

The Convoy of Death

The counter-selective processes that National Socialism saw being incubated in the people were thought to be a result of urban life. Heritable traits that had crystallized through ancestral selective criteria, such as the will to fight against the environment, heroism and creativity in survival methods, were diminished in the comfort of the city, hidden among the concrete and skyscrapers. In spite of this, National Socialism did not intend to turn the community toward a kind of pastoral romanticism, but rather aimed at appeasing counter-selection through a cultural change that eliminated urban ethics. "This does not mean becoming peasants again, but resisting the urbanization of feeling, which tends to stray from the *Life-Laws*.[103]

Birth studies carried out by the SS through its "Office of Family Affairs" (*Sippenamt*) had shown that countryside-to-city migration, necessary for the industrialization of the *Reich*, brought with it higher birthrates, a marked deterioration of the quality of life and the attenuation of selection. An article by Jost Fritz, a contributor to the *Guidance Notebooks* for SS leaders, reported on the damaging results of the rural exodus. The migration from the countryside to the cities was called by Fritz, "the convoy of death". By 1939, the year his work was published, the cities of the Reich were failing to provide even half of the births necessary to maintain the population, despite marked efforts to increase those rates through public policy. The rural sectors, on the other hand, had a surplus of 13%, having become the *Reich's* source of life. The city, in the National Socialist Worldview, was a kind of "people's cemetery".

One of the scientists most committed to stopping the counter-selective process acting upon urban man was Konrad Lorenz. The ethologist, member of the NSDAP and future Nobel Prize winner, was promptly hired as an advisor to Gross's Office of Racial Policy. For Ute Deichmann, author of a comprehensive analysis of the study and practice of biology during the Nazi period, Konrad Lorenz not only

---

SS-Hauptamt
103 Army Personnel Office. *Why Do We Fight?*

brought about a revolutionary change in behavioral psychology, he was also fundamental in giving a scientific basis to the Nazi struggle to reverse counter-selective processes.

> Lorenz denounced degenerative genetic changes in the sphere of instinctive behavior, caused by domestication as well as the civilizing process. He perceived in the over-civilization of urban man a series of hereditary traits typical of domesticated animals. Lorenz rejected the Spenglerian pessimism that denied any possibility of progress. For Lorenz, decay was a biological problem. The great number of degenerative types whose number increased under civilization was the result of domestication.[104]

For Lorenz, "a change in environmental influences, the elimination and in certain cases radical reversal of selection" were the cause of what National Socialism had noted as a serious physiological decline. Food problems, the repression of instincts, problems regulating sexuality, infantile regression, and parental dependence, were just some of the harmful effects found by Lorenz to affect men living sheltered, comfortable, civilized lives. In order to reverse these processes Lorenz proposed a selection based on the criteria of tenacity and heroism;

> if we don't, a humanity deprived of natural selection will be annihilated by degeneration.[105]

Lorenz believed that normal preservationist instincts were undone in populations living under the false security, shelter, and comfort of urban life. The more harsh conditions were alleviated, the further this instinct was diluted. Through a correct attitude towards selection under more traditional criteria, this physiological degeneration could be reversed, even in large cities.

> Selection favoring resistance, heroism, [and] social sacrifice, is the foundation of our form of government. From the beginning,

---

104 Ute Deichmann. *Biologists under Hitler*
105 Lorenz quoted by Ute Deichmann

the Movement opposed the domestication of humanity. It is true that socialism and communism could draw from a twisted kind of Darwinism, which erroneously considers humanity as a whole to be a unit of value. But the evidence that value is given equitably only in racial groups, and not in all humanity, transforms socialism into National Socialism.

FOUNTAIN OF LIFE

Nazism held the only source of natural selection left to the *Reich* to be in the old peasantry. The source of life and quarry of selection was in those populations still attached to agricultural life, outdoor health and permanent contact with the environment and the *Life-Laws*.

Plans for physiological renewal were based on this source of life. This reserve of natural selection was called the new nobility of "Blood and Soil" (*Blut und Boden*). A new legal system was established for its revitalization based on ancestral selective criteria, the so-called Odalic Right. Walther Darré, SS General (*SS-Obergruppenführer*), Minister of Food and Agriculture and director of the SS Race and Settlement Main Office (RuSHA), was responsible for this biological renewal plan.

> The true notion of nobility, in the Germanic sense, is characterized by the selection of consciously educated leaders based on certain hereditary nuclei. The ancient German nobility enjoyed no public privileges or rights over the other men of the tribe, nor were they granted any more than a de facto priority. Their influence was only based on the respect that the people had for those elite families. We need, in any event, to return to the Germanic concept of nobility. From the day we had a solid and scientific doctrine of heredity, we have seen though the prejudices of all the distinctions of social classes based on any criteria other than the hereditary value of blood. The most modern and least backward branch of our sciences, biology, automatically brings us back to the old Germanic idea. The new nobility must once again be a living source of scrupulously

chosen chiefs. We must provide it with the means to preserve by inheritance the blood that has proved its worth, to eliminate the blood of inferior quality and to allow it to appropriate, if necessary, any valuable new characteristics which might emerge from the people.[106]

Günther Pacyna, SS officer and contributor to the *Guidance Notebooks*, emphasized the *Reich* leadership's intention to link old peasant law to new racial legislation.

The heads of the National Socialist State have consciously developed the law regarding the agricultural heritage of the Reich on the basis of hereditary law, which finds its origin in the law of the State.[107]

The *SS-Hauptsturmführer* Ernst Scharper came to base the whole policy of creating a new elite of leaders, the so-called "Leader principle" (*Führerprinzip*), on the selective tradition of the peasantry.

The clan held the source of rural life, nourished by a hereditary position indissolubly linked to ancestry. The product of the camp, the *Odal*, was the absolute foundation of every legitimate German, both the chief and the warrior. Since ethnic communities were composed only of peasants, peasant leaders were also the people's chiefs. Neither the confrontation with the Roman world, nor emigrations, nor even the glory and joy of fighting destroyed the peasant roots of the Germans.[108]

One of the practical achievements of this selective policy was the "Law of the Hereditary Farm" (*Erbhof Gesetz*), a legal order that created a new category of agricultural land. An honorary title was also created for the peasants. Those peasants who fulfilled the conditions of hereditary health and maintained an attachment to the land could choose the title

---

106 Walther Darre. *Race. A New Nobility Based on Blood and Soil*
107 Günther Pacyna. *Basic law of the peasantry, Guidance Notebooks, SS-Hauptamt*
108 Ernst Scharper. *German Authority, Guidance Notebooks, SS-Hauptamt*

of peasant (*Bauer*). This new nobility possessed no wealth other than its biological heritage and a piece of land protected by the state for use in agricultural work. The *Erbhof* was a true agrarian order. With the *Erbhof* law a central office was established that guided and controlled the entire agricultural production and distribution chain. All efforts were united under one centralized and streamlined system, under the purview of the "Office of Nutrition Control" (*Reichnahrstand*, RNS). The *Erbhof* law, the *Bauer* farmers and the RNS were the basis of a new elite based on the pockets of rural populations that were, to some extent, immune to the processes of counter-selection.

THE FÜHRER PRINCIPLE

But National Socialism could not base its plan of selective renewal only on rural populations who were separated from political and social life, but had to include the community as a whole. For all types of populations National Socialism devised a plan of biological renewal that included the creation of new selective population pockets through elite organizations. Entry into these organizations began with a basic selection, based on parameters of racial metrics, health and ability, but once within these bodies, the candidate began a process of ascent through the hierarchies of the *Reich,* according to the meritocratic leader principle (*Führerprinzip*). Rising up the leadership chain was predicated on capacity for leadership, inventiveness and willpower.

> The best State constitution and State form is that which, with the most natural certainty, brings the best members of the national community to leading importance and to leading influence.[109]

The leader principle carried out selection by handing great responsibilities to chiefs and leaders, who had to solve these problems imaginatively, and in an autonomous, independent way. For this reason the leaders (*Führers*) were endowed with full powers and responsibility to carry out tasks in the most independent and non-bureaucratic possible way. The *Führerprinzip* created an elite with a

---

109 Hitler. *Mein Kampf*

strong sense of autonomy, a body that rejected the old hierarchical and bureaucratic government order. Franz Neumann, a scholar who traversed the Nazi *Reich,* reported on what he considered to be an egalitarian and virtually anti-hierarchical elite.

> We also know that many of the hierarchic orders have fallen to pieces, not only in the army but also in the civil service. The soldier or non-commissioned officer, if entrusted with a task, is responsible to himself alone and need not tolerate any interference by any superior save the one who has issued the command. National Socialist cells in the civil service break down the barriers between the academic and non-academic civil services... Officers and soldiers consort socially, privates need no longer rise and stand at attention when officers enter a restaurant. The S.A. and the S.S. are pseudo-egalitarian bodies; so is the army on a larger scale.*[110]*

This Nazi egalitarianism was very different from socialist egalitarianism. For Nazism, selection could not be subject to privileges. It needed the largest number of individuals in order to extend the sample subject to selection, hence the rejection of the structured order in social classes and in the differences in opportunities when proving value and capacity.

> Formerly, superior talent was taken as a social privilege. In the National Socialist State, selection is not based on social class, but on skill. The National Socialist Educational Institutes, the Adolf Hitler Schools and the Castles of the Order are proof of this. Their graduates will be the leaders of the *Reich*. We are convinced that heritable factors determine for the highest and longest-lasting accomplishments. We, therefore, put forward the idea of selection as primary.*[111]*

In a celebrated speech to the NSDAP middle-rank commanders

---
110 Franz Neumann. *Behemoth: the Structure and Practice of National Socialism*
111 SS-Hauptamt. *SS-Man and Blood Questions*

(*Kreisleiter*) at the Vogelsang political training school, Hitler spoke of his plan for selective renewal to confront the crisis of Western man. In the speech, the *Führer* brought the concept of the natural selection together with artificial selection, and explained how a political organization should echo the *Life-Laws* by replicating the natural order in society. Hitler launched into a harsh criticism of the Western democracies, which he described as counter-selective and causing a crisis of talent in the conduct of European peoples. "In the National Socialist Reich, parents know that their children will achieve the status owed to them by their personal talents. No child will be held back by the social or economic position of its parents. It is National Socialism that has set out to train these future leaders. Its mission is to draw from the masses a ruling elite who will govern with toughness and ensure the continued existence of our way of life. This goal requires selecting the best. The ranks of the Party are composed of the brave, the gifted, the honest, and the idealistic.

In looking to the future, we know this selection process must continue—a process that occurs naturally in the struggle for power. The selection process begins at a young age. Difficult tests must be administered to all of the many boys gifted in politics. In democracy, this selection becomes inverted. Heroism is foolish, since parliamentarianism is based on the overestimation of the isolated individual, and for said individual, heroism and sacrifice are but prejudices. That is why the spirit of sacrifice and responsibility in democracies is a fault, something bad. In these democracies, the community is relegated to the background. An authentic democrat is always a pacifist and they never sacrifice themselves, although they always expect some fool to do it for them. This way of thinking must end once and for all. In the organic State and its Community there are many more opportunities for talent to emerge. These do not endanger the boss, as in a democracy, where the boss thinks they will replace him. In the National Socialist State, on the contrary, the boss supports these emerging talents and surrounds himself with brilliant collaborators, and only those who are obedient and loyal will receive obedience and loyalty when his turn comes. Believe me, the current crisis of democracies will only be overcome with real leaders. Those that will emerge from a search within the people, through a process of selection, the best of whom will go on to occupy key positions." [112]

THE ORDER OF THE CLANS

One could say that National Socialism sought to promote the selection criteria through two mechanisms. The first was supposed to restore the social actor which preserved a selective tradition throughout history. That actor was the rural family. The second mechanism was the creation of a new social actor that would safeguard selection criteria. An artificial, political social actor, created under the National Socialist State and fostered by both the rural and urban populations. This new elite would be the leaders of the Movement, and especially the leaders of the families or clans of the SS. From this group Hitler sought to take the intellectual and ruling elite of the Reich.

> I do not doubt for a moment, despite certain people's skepticism, that within a hundred or so years from now all the German élite will be a product of the SS—for only the SS practices racial selection.[113]

The Order of the Clans (*Sippenorden*) of the SS was the group of SS families, with heritable characteristics to some extent sheltered from biological counter-selective processes, that comprised the SS troops and their immediate families. For the SS, success in selection was not guaranteed by recruiting exceptional individuals, but only by recruiting complete families, clans and creating an entirely exceptional community.

> The SS does not aspire to a privileged position within the people. It is an Order that by its fighting action serves to facilitate racial selection within the community. Thus, the SS applies a fundamental law of our socialist value scale, that demands that each one occupy his place according to the value of the results

---
112 Hitler. *Kreisleiter Speech in Vogelsang, 1937*
113 Hitler. *Table Talk*

The Law of Selection

obtained in the bosom of the popular community. The SS clearly sees that in pursuing these goals, it must be more than just a men's club (Männerbund). The SS bases its ideas of the Order on the clan community. It wants to be an Order of Clans that will see the men of the best Nordic type born to serve the Reich. In this way, selection will not judge the lone individual but the value of an entire clan.[114]

The Order of the Clans was to be the elite of the Reich's selection. Himmler was aware that for this reason the phenotypic aspect was not the only metric to be used, especially considering the dynamics of recessive factors. *"What looks healthy on the outside can conceal diseased elements on the inside"*[115]. A Nordic elite, like Himmler wanted to make up his Order of Clans, did not mean an elite that was satisfied with the Nordic appearance. The Nordic race for the SS meant appearance and attitude, physical and mental health and many times those parameters could not be found all together.

There are two ways to enter the SS. The first way was through war and the struggle for existence. In the year when the SS was formed, there were still many veterans whose value could be ascertained through their service record. Wars, however, are exceptional circumstances and we had to find a selection formula for peacetime, when courage is not put to the test. One could only judge by appearances. Obviously everyone will be able to argue that it is very problematic only to look at blue eyes, blond hair and cranial measurements. This is evident to me as well. You can never judge just by that. With this outward appearance, then, it was not possible to make a final definitive selection, since the person's performance through the months and years is always important to consider.[116]

The SS was the organization within the Movement called by Hitler

---
114 Anonymous. The SS as Order. *Guidance Notebooks*, SS-Hauptamt
115 Hauptamt-SS. *SS Mate Selection and Race*
116 Heinrich Himmler. *Speech to the Wehrmacht Officers' Corps, 1937*

to lead the selective processes aimed at the physiological and cultural renewal of the Nazi Reich. For the SS, selection was Hitler's most revolutionary idea, even more than political measures or even the Jewish question.

> From the beginning the following principle was affirmed by the SS: numerical limitation and extreme selection! The leadership in Munich never tried to gather as many men as possible, but it emphasized the excellent quality of the men they chose. Like the farmer who, having from a more or less good old seed that must be carefully sifted, goes to the field to collect the first shoots, we have rejected out of hand the men that we thought we could not use to build of the SS Troop. The Reichsführer has the extreme merit of having followed this path with courage and a persuasive spirit, for at that time even in the ranks of the Movement the racial question was still a totally obscure notion. For the first time, the racial question was at the center of concerns, differing widely from the natural, but negative, hatred of the Jew. The *Führer's* most revolutionary idea was taking shape. With the laws that we have passed we want to ensure that not every son of an SS family has the right to be a member of the SS, only some of the children of those families will be admitted. The result obtained so far is nothing more than a sketch. The creation of a human elite must be consistent and limitless, for there is not a standard SS. Each generation of SS must be better than the previous one.[117]

---

117 Anonymous. The SS Order, *History And Principles. Guidance Notebooks*, SS-Hauptamt

Fertility Law

The *Law of Fertility* (Gesetz der Fruchtbarkeit) was intimately linked to selection. For National Socialism, fertility referred to a universal order, a natural economy which found its utmost expression in ensuring value and, therefore, evolutionary success. This natural economy, abundant and fecund, encompassed not only the quantitative but also the qualitative. The Nazis argued that, in nature, more individuals were more likely to contain valuable elements than fewer individuals. In humans, the more individuals of value the greater the chances of an inventive genius appearing. With more individuals the selection processes would be more assertive, because fertility allowed for a greater number of heritable traits, which widened the spectrum of selection possibilities.

According to the Nazi fertility law, the more hereditary characteristics nature had at its disposal to select, the more value the preserved genes would have.

> When the community restricts its fertility and adopts the system of one or two children, the biological consequences are serious, as they affect the process of selecting the best.[118]

The value of heritable characteristics derived precisely from being selected from among the greatest number of possibilities, according to the criterion of their usefulness in the struggle for existence. For National Socialism no one should be exempted from the *Law of Fertility*, since, with a correct mate selection policy, all combinations of traits and ways of interacting with the environment were worth putting to the test of their value in the struggle for existence.

---

118 Hitler. *Speech before cadets and officers in the Sportpalaz, 1940*

In the Nazi Worldview, fertility ensured value in selection, which resulted in a greater capacity for struggle.

> The individual's life disappears completely in the evolution of the species. We only need to recognize natural events and act accordingly. What our ancestors understood instinctively, that one must be strongly united to nature, must again become common knowledge. The individual does not matter, only the preservation of the species. Life is eternal struggle. An individual's death does not affect the essence of selection, because valuable inheritable traits are only gradually eliminated when they are not significantly transferred. In the next generation, these characteristics will not be sufficiently represented, and will further fade away. The person who does not have children may live longer but will be expelled forever from the race life. His genetic characteristics combined with his environment conditions are unique. The permanence of individual achievements is only assured if the creative person is perpetuated in the works of his descendants. Only fertility determines the continuation of its heritable constitution.[119]

Fertility and Politics

For National Socialism fertility was a law of nature that was confirmed again and again among the earth's organisms. The struggle for existence was hard, and nature produced abundance as a defense mechanism.

> The enormous abundance that is found in nature is explained by the evident destruction of a great amount of individual beings. Prospects for survival in the world are not the same for all living things. Abundance and fertility are a precondition to guarantee the maintenance of a type of organism, and thus prevent its extinction.[120]

---

119 SS-Hauptamt. *Believe and fight*
120 SS-Hauptamt. *SS-Man and Blood Questions*

Fertility Law

For Nazism, one of the most characteristic symptoms of counter-selective ideologies and the waning of the *Life-Laws* was the birth shortage. When ideologies of this type were adopted, hundreds of thousands of years of efforts oriented to maximum fertility and creative strength suddenly stopped. National Socialism assumed man must be greatly abstracted from his natural inheritance if that instinct, present in all the other organisms of earth, were inhibited.

> Animals and plants produce more offspring than is necessary for survival. The seedling plant produces 4,000 seeds. If all of them grew and reproduced, after 5 years there would be 256,000,000,000,000 flowers. By the sixth year they would not fit on the surface of the planet. A single codfish contains 4 million eggs. The enormous fertility of nature is understood when we consider the enormous destruction of individuals. The number of cribs must be greater than the number of coffins. Abundance is the prerequisite for the preservation of a sufficient number of creatures, so that the species does not perish. Without abundance there is no evolution.[121]

The shortage of births represented, in the eyes of National Socialism, a claudication in the struggle for existence, one of the causes of peoples' death. This is because periods of hardship had always entailed greater fertility, which resulted in better selection and, therefore, in better individuals.

> The survival of the species depends on the growth rate. The lower the number of offspring, the more in danger is the species' existence. This is why animal species whose offspring live in particularly dangerous conditions breed a large number of offspring.[122].

Hardness in the struggle was synonymous with fertility, this translated to better selection, which resulted in individuals better-endowed and therefore better-adapted.

---

[121] SS-Hauptamt. S*S Mate Selection and Race*
[122] Eduard Paul Tratz. *Struggle in Nature, Guidance Notebooks, SS-Hauptamt*

Dr. SS Gerhard Schinke thought of the fertility law as one of the most sensitive when it comes to the survival of peoples. For the SS official, adhering to the fertility law would allow the eternal survival of a human group. Schinke thus confronted conservative cultural pessimism which, following the historian Spengler, insisted that other organic laws, superior to the fertility law and the *Law of Selection*, could determine the life cycle of organisms:

> Germany can die in spite of its power and its present splendor. History teaches us that people can disappear, since from the time they exist they are responsible for themselves and their survival. Just ten years ago, there were people who even believed in an inevitable disappearance of the nation. Oswald Spengler's prophecy that the West was bound to perish was accepted by the weak and cowardly who no longer had faith in life. Spengler stated: 'According to an internal law, every people and culture must die one day, after having gone through their youth and maturity!' But his comparison between the people's destiny and the tree's, or the individual's, is wrong. For the existence of the individual is limited, he ages and he must die. The isolated tree grows and dies and yet, the forests are eternal. The isolated man also lives and must disappear, and yet peoples are eternal. Peoples should not die like a man or an isolated tree, but they run the risk of dying. Doom, unfathomable fate was not the reason for the death of the civilized peoples of antiquity. They violated divine laws. The peoples who have disappeared in the course of history are those who have disregarded the wisdom and the laws of nature.

> An examination of the numerical and qualitative evolution of the German people in the course of recent years shows that he too has irresponsibly and unconcernedly transgressed the iron *Life-Laws*. The most disadvantaged families almost always have more children than well-off families. It was not, therefore, misery and worry that prevented births, but the love of comfort, selfish reasoning, and cowardice in the struggle for existence, the fear of having to reduce pleasures and luxury. The will to

have a child, or rather to have many children, is necessary for all of us SS men, since the German people should not die, but must be eternal.[123]

For National Socialism, one of the most urgent counter-selective processes to combat was the birth shortage. The ordinance laws of the SS were explicit on this point. Fritz Weitzel, SS General (*SS-Obergruppenführer*) and author of official texts on the NS Worldview restates this point in all his works. "The issue of having many children is not a private matter, but a duty to our ancestors and our people. Four is the minimum number of children in a healthy SS marriage. In the case of some misfortune of destiny that prevents a marriage from producing children, the SS Leader *(SS-Führer)* must adopt children of racial and genetic value in order to educate them in the National Socialist sense"[124]

Marriage and family, during the National Socialist Reich, were not aims in themselves as in conservative ideologies, marriage according to the biological Worldview was a valid institution because it facilitated conception. During the Nazi Reich, young marriages were promoted and enormous resources were provided to provoke an abundance of children. But if marriage was not at the service of procreation, the Nazi State had no qualms about granting divorces. Weikart relates in his book on Hitler's ethics that in 1939, before the beginning of the war and the inevitable loss of human lives, Himmler exhorted his officers to procreate inside or outside marriage. Rudolf Hess unleashed a furious controversy by publicly proposing the same thing, and Hitler was not afraid of going in the same direction.

The Nazis advocated early marriage, relaxed the divorce laws in cases of infertility or irreconcilable ruptures, approved of extramarital sex, and tried to erase the stigma of illegitimacy. Hitler wanted more births and did not care about the traditional role of women. Whether they worked in industry, offices or

---
123 Gerhart Schinke. What do peoples die of? I. The Decline of Birthrates, *Guidance Notebooks*, SS-Hauptamt
124 Fritz Weitzel. *Laws of the SS Order.* SS-Hauptamt.

stayed at home did not matter. However, he did not authorize their conscription because he thought it might lower the birth rate. Here we see another example of a political inconsistency but one which is nevertheless explained by the Worldview.[125]

Such was the importance given to fertility that the policies of National Socialism allocated important resources to promote it. These subsidies were made from the first day of government, even though the most urgent need was finding work for six million unemployed people, not to increase material needs with new burdens. Enormous sums of public money were spent on stimulating young marriages and procreation, with the foreknowledge that the fruits of these policies would be reflected in the decades to come. Rudolf Frercks, *SS-Obersturmbannführer* and deputy director of the "NS-Racial Policy Office" detailed the government's efforts in this area:

> Since 1918, Germany has suffered a decline in its birth rate that far exceeds the human losses of the World War. The number of voluntary abortions grew dramatically, and the resulting health disturbances often resulted in years of illness for women. Late marriage and singleness were the fatal cause of a reverse selection, the loss of valuable and intelligent men. The overvaluation of education and the insane eagerness to ascend socially were two of the main reasons for restricting births in the highest sectors of the population.
>
> The number of births in 1900 was 37 per 1,000 and in 1933 only 14.7 per 1,000. Dr. Burgdörfer, director of the National Statistics Center, has calculated that for the conservation of the people, 22 births per 1,000 inhabitants are needed in one year. In nature, there is everywhere a right and an obligation not imposed by man but inherent to all beings. It is the right to the conservation of the species. It is, therefore, perfectly natural for the new Germany to be concerned with the preservation of its existence and to devote its attention and care to it. 'I measure,' says Hitler,

---

125 Richard Weikart. *Hitler's Ethic*

Fertility Law

'the success of our work not in the growth of our roads. I do not measure it in our new factories, I do not measure it either in the new bridges we build or by the divisions we enlist. The true deciding factor in the success of our work is the German youth. If the youth increases in number, then I know that our people will not perish, and that our work has not been sterile.'

On June 1, 1933, the law for the promotion of marriage was passed. Young people who want to get married can apply to their municipalities for a loan without interest. The loan is not made in money, but in the form of purchase bonds for housing and household goods. With each child born in these marriages, the loan is reduced by 25%. With four children, the loan is forgiven. As of April 1, 1938, 900,000 marriage loans had been granted. On the other hand, the father of a family has to worry about a thousand day-to-day things that one who does not have children, does not need to worry about. Many times in the struggle for existence he has to yield to others and he is not, therefore, in the same conditions to compete.

The National Socialist state knows that having many children should not lead to the impoverishment of families, because exactly these large families guarantee the future of the people and the State for the coming days. That is why some measures have already been taken, of which we shall mention the most important. Subsidies for poor families where there are at least four children under the age of sixteen.

As of April 1, 1938, these subsidies were granted to 560,000 needy families with 3 million children altogether. This measure was extended in August 1936 by granting a regular subsidy for the third and fourth child, with 20 additional marks for the fifth child and each subsequent child under twenty-one years. The granting of this subsidy is limited only to those whose income does not exceed 8,000 marks a year. Thus, a worker with eight children who earns 160 marks per month will receive, from the State, 100 marks per paycheck every month. This amount is not subject to any tax. So far, this regular subsidy has been paid to about 2 million children. Also, in order to determine the salary tax, reductions corresponding to the children have been implemented and the usual financial differences between the unmarried and the married are diminishing. There are further proposals for tax and expense reductions, according to the number of children, which represent the principle of a general compensation for childbirth and which will definitively end the economic privilege of those who do not have children.[126]

Fertility and Inventive Genius

For Hitler and National Socialism, fertility and abundant procreation allowed the preservation of the community and the transmission of successful heritable traits on the evolutionary path. Having many children ensured the vitality of peoples and protected them from aging and extinction.

> The child, this tiny creature who must come into being, is the sole purpose of the whole struggle for life.[127]

But the fear of low fertility was not only about quantitative problems. In the eyes of the NS Worldview, a drop in birth rate directly affected the qualitative aspects of selective processes. In the National Socialist Worldview, abundance and fertility were the basis of selection and this was understood as the foundation for creating physiological value and cultural progress. When fertility was low, selection had to be made within a much narrower range of heritable characteristics. When fertility was extremely low there was no possibility of selection and all heritable traits, both advantageous and unfavorable, were transferred.

> As soon as the procreative faculty is thwarted and the number of births diminished, the natural struggle for existence, which allows only healthy and strong individuals to survive is replaced

---

126 Rudolf Frercks. *German Population Policy*
127 Hitler. *Address to the National Socialist Women's Organization, 1939*

Fertility Law

by a sheer craze to 'save' feeble, and even diseased, creatures at any cost. Thus are sown the seeds of a human progeny which will become more and more enfeebled from one generation to another, as long as Nature's will is scorned.[128]

Low fertility, then, affected not only evolutionary paths and adaptive capacity. The biological or organic vision of culture that the Nazis had gave precedence to the selection law in the cultural planes as well. As indicated by the National Socialist selection law, defective selection processes led to cultural decay resulting from the dearth of valuable men. Thus the National Socialist insistence on emphasizing fertility and selection went hand in hand with their plan to re-evaluate human capital. The more individuals were born, the more chances of greater men.

If we had practiced the system of two children per family in antiquity, Germany would have been deprived of its greatest geniuses. Why is it that exceptional men in families are often the fifth, seventh, tenth or even twelfth child?[129]

Ensuring the highest quality of these processes was the key to evolutionary success and the creation of a superior culture.

One ought to realize that for one Goethe, Nature may bring into existence ten thousand such scribblers who act as the worst kind of germ-carriers in poisoning human souls.[130]

For National Socialism, if the State had the will, neither Spenglerian cycles nor cosmic curses could restrain the biological renewal of man. It was only necessary to stop counter-selection and re-establish the laws of existence to experience a cultural and physiological flowering.

In fact, we do not believe that the time of creative energy, of

---

128 Hitler. *Mein Kampf*
129 Hitler. *Table Talk*
130 Hitler. *Mein Kampf*

unique personalities of genius, has been exhausted with the great men of the past centuries, that we are witnessing the emergence of an era marked by the mud of the collective! No, we are convinced that precisely at this time, when we regard the individual creations of the highest level in so many sectors, that the highest values of personality will be revealed anew, and victoriously.[131]

In this sense, Nietzsche was the great prophet of the inherent abundance of nature and of the creative man as its reflection. Nietzschean biologism was replete with analogies of those men of superior spirit, bearers of abundance and inventive genius. For Nietzsche these creative geniuses and active spirits were bearers of what he called the "Great Economy of Life" (*Grosse Ökonomie des Lebens*), a natural force that would tend to abundance and fertility. *"The overall aspect of life is not the dire situation, not starvation, but rather riches, profusion, even absurd waste."*[132]. This abundance present in nature was for Nietzsche a force that tended to waste resources in order to reach the maximum number of possibilities in generating value and improvement. That internal abundance was translated into fecundity and progeny, creative inventiveness and the fertility of ideas.

Nietzsche's criticism of his time, and especially of the intellectual elite, pointed at all times to the weakening of man's creative capacity, that capacity for overflowing superfluity and true inner value, which is characteristic of free spirits and healthy economies.

> The present age is not one of complete and mature personalities, but of the utmost utility. The words market, supply, industry, profitability and any other word defined by selfishness come to our lips to speak of the recent generation of intellectuals.[133]

For Nietzsche, the mercantile society was constantly attacking the

---

131 Hitler. *Opening Speech of the First Great Exhibition of German Art*
132 Nietzsche. *Twilight of the Idols*
133 Nietzsche. *Schopenhauer as an educator*

source of these creative geniuses.

> Another human type becomes ever more disadvantaged and is finally made impossible; above all, the great 'architects': the strength to build is now paralyzed; the courage to make far-reaching plans is discouraged; the organizational geniuses become scarce; who still dares to undertake works that would require millennia to complete?[134]

For Nietzsche, the mercantile era, despite being an economic epoch, did not know how to use this precious human capital. A society obsessed with the idea of accumulation absurdly acted in the opposite way. *"Our age may talk of economy, but it is in fact a squanderer. It squanders the most precious thing there is, the spirit"*[135]

For Nietzsche, it was precisely these creators and bearers of abundance who had allowed for the development and progress of nations, through "Creative Destruction." In this process the creators follow their essence; they are instruments of abundance and of the *Will to Power*. That tendency was a passion, a powerful instinct that in the Germanic cultural sphere was expressed in creative inventiveness and technological development. Everything that the creative man assimilated was transformed to produce something new, that is why the Nietzschean creator did not manufacture from nothing, but produced through the transformation and rearrangement of the energies of nature, destroying ancient creations with the creation of new ones.

Nietzsche's *creative man* was responsible for the technological renewal of history through the destruction generated by new ideas. "The strongest spirits are those who have so far done the most to advance humanity: time and again they rekindled the dozing passions... reawakened the sense of delight in what is new, daring, unattempted; They forced men to pit opinion against opinion, ideal model against ideal model, mostly by force of arms, by toppling boundary stones,

---
134 Nietzsche. *The Gay Science*
135 Nietzsche. *Daybreak*

by violating pieties—but also by means of new religions and moralities!"[136] "Creative Destruction" was the free unfolding of the *Will to Power*, a creative force that forged its path by destroying old limits. "Whoever wants to be a creator must first be a destroyer"[137]

For Nietzsche, abundance was the reflection of the *Will to Power*, the will to preserve and overcome, the only way to succeed mediocrity and standardization.

> The amazing economy of the preservation of the species, an economy that is certainly costly, wasteful, and on the whole, most foolish, but still *proven* to have preserved our race thus far.[138]

For Nietzsche, creative genius was costly, the product of the trial and error of many generations and the effort to maintain an ever-renewed improvement and increase in value. Nietzsche thought, like National Socialism, that abundance hid a tension of creative forces that sooner or later exploded to consummate themselves in great achievements.

> Great men, like great epochs, are explosive material in whom tremendous energy has been accumulated... If the tension in the mass has grown too great, the merest accidental stimulus suffices to call the 'genius', the 'deed', the great destiny, into the world. Take the case of Napoleon.[139]

In the Nietzschean "Great Economy", creation and transformation derived from preservation and improvement.

> Creating, that is the great salvation from suffering, and life's alleviation. But for the creator to appear, suffering itself is needed, and much transformation. Yea, much bitter dying must there be in your lives, you creators! Thus are you advocates

---

136 Nietzsche. *The Gay Science*
137 Nietzsche. *Thus Spoke Zarathustra*
138 Nietzsche. *The Gay Science*
139 Nietzsche. *Twilight of the Idols*.

and justifiers of all perishableness... Evil do I call it and misanthropic: all that teaching about the one, and the plenum, and the unmoved, and the sufficient and the imperishable![140]

The man who was not creative or influenced by natural fertility became a source of scarcity. He fell prey to the mania to reflect upon everything with neutrality, to the impoverishment of the will, to a loss of capital, impoverished senses, corruption, exhaustion, the will to nothingness (Christianity, Buddhism, nihilism), weakness, moralism, fear, and mediocrity. For Nietzsche, the exceptional men and bearers of abundance could not contain their inner wealth.

I am weary of my wisdom, like the bee that has gathered too much honey; I need hands outstretched to take it. I need to give and give. Bless the cup that is about to overflow, that the water may flow golden out of it, and carry everywhere the reflection of your bliss![141]

These superman creators were the real engine of the "Great Economy" of human existence and their action meant fertile and overflowing wealth.

In this condition (ecstatic intoxication), one enriches everything out of one's own abundance: what one sees, what one desires, one sees swollen, pressing, strong, overladen with energy. The man in ecstasy transforms things until they mirror his power – until they are reflections of his perfection.[142]

Artist and Soldier

For Nazism, counter-selective ideologies were an attack on the laws of nature which produced scarcity, they were a cultural plague. Biological shortages, low birth rates, leadership crises and men without will,

---
140 Nietzsche. *Thus Spoke Zarathustra*
141 Nietzsche. *Thus Spoke Zarathustra*
142 Nietzsche. *Twilight of the Idols*

economies that brought inequality and a general poverty of spirit were the sign of an era of ontological scarcity and the exhaustion of man's most precious capital. This irreducible human value came from a capital other than money, what Nietzsche called "Capital of Intelligence and Will" (*Geist und Willenskapital*).

National Socialism echoed the Nietzschean call for man to be a bearer of the energy of creative abundance. The inventive genius, the organizer, the forger of historical destiny, was a creator, an artist capable of molding the mutable clay of the world to achieve monumental goals. They were the great men, the bearers of the inherent abundance of nature. The SS took this Nietzschean concept of the power of the creative force and developed it as a method to endow their elite troops with strength and hardness. For Nazism, creativity and inventive genius were the fruit of selection, just as hardness and ability were the fruits of struggle. The Nazi warrior had to be creative, with an abundant artistic spirit. In the Nazi Worldview, natural biological selection meant the selection of men who were inventive geniuses and innate leaders.

> There was a time when military spirit and art were considered incompatible. But the attentive observer will not be surprised by the fact that our greatest soldiers have possessed an artistic nature. Adolf Hitler, artist and soldier, has etched with a bronze dagger the outlines of the idea that will govern the millennium: National Socialism. The SS, the Fuhrer's Order, which must represent the warlike aspect of our Worldview, likewise feels called to participate actively in artistic creation. The reason for this is the creative nature behind National Socialism.[143]

For the shock troops of National Socialism, the warrior was an artist, since both were fed by the same source of natural abundance. Their descriptions of the transfiguration produced by combat and the warrior force were strikingly coincident with Nietzschean poetry on the inner goods of creative abundance.

---

143 Anonymous. The Artists and the SS. *Guidance Notebooks*, SS-Hauptamt

Fertility Law

> When the warrior in battle has overcome all weakness, have you not suddenly felt a force previously unknown? It is like the breaking of a chain in which one has always been bound, one escapes and feels like God or a child. There are no hesitations, no doubts, no considerations. The soldier, who faces death, is a free man. There is a kinship of a creative nature between soldier and artist. A soldier from the front writes: 'One day I will express what my heart hides in this wartime hour. I want to become a gold seeker in my own heart, transmit everything I see and enrich all men'. This relationship between artist and soldier is what allows us, comrades, to enter into a new relationship with true art, the only art worthy of you. We will one day reap the fruits of having lived through difficult times, where we strive to understand the great art, comparable in the aspect we assume in the moment of the most dangerous fighting. We will find treasures which we did not suspect until now.[144]

The archetype of the new Nazi man was a product of the most rigorous selection, a fertility-bearing warrior, expressed in abundant offspring, fertility of ideas, overflowing leadership and artistic creativity, analogies of the Great Economy of Life.

Fertility and Economy

With its plan to restore the *Life-Laws*, National Socialism confronted the economic theories indicated by Nietzsche as bringers of scarcity. The capitalist and Marxist economies were seen as counter-selective, which is why Nazism had to develop an alternative economic path, a praxis that abandoned the dogmatic theories that set aside Nietzsche's human capital of will and intelligence.

According to Nazi logic, the economy served only as an administrator of natural wealth and human value. In the Nazi Worldview, all economic capital came from biology and not from the gold standard or from the management of variables such as income, employment,

---

[144] Hans Klöcket. Artist and Soldier. *Guidance Notebooks*, SS-Hauptamt

balance of payments or the behavior of prices, derivatives that in the Reich did not have much economic prominence.

The economy is for National Socialism an objective sought for higher purposes, a system of means directed to an end. Economic life is morally linked to and an expression of the soul-life. With the methodology of the economic-scientific research of the present, one cannot learn the new concept of the economy, since the economic is not a matter of purely economic causes, quite the opposite, all the values of nationality belong also to the economic. The new economic policy, therefore, must never consider immediate profitability, but must be occupied in the long run with people's well-being for generations. To understand the economic doctrine of National Socialism, an organic conception of economics, it is necessary, in principle, to explain the fundamental ideas of the Worldview of National Socialism.[145]

The economic policy of National Socialism had no dogmas. Its objectives were subordinated to success in the struggle for existence. Otto Nathan, a professor at Princeton University and a contemporary of Nazism, began his research on the National Socialist financial system by rejecting any attempt to classify Nazi economic theory. "Nazism erected a system of production, distribution and consumption that defies classification in any of the usual categories. It was not capitalism in the traditional sense: the autonomous market mechanism so characteristic of capitalism during the last two centuries had all but disappeared. It was not State capitalism: the government disclaimed any desire to own the means of production, and in fact took steps to denationalize them. It was not socialism or communism: private property and private profit still existed. The Nazi system was, rather, a combination of some of the characteristics of capitalism and a highly planned economy...Commodity prices, interest rates, and wages were not only fixed by the government, but they lost completely their traditional significance as regulators of economic activity"

---

[145] Arthur Reinhold Hermann and Arthur Ritsch. *Economics in the National Socialist Worldview*

Franz Neumann, a renowned German political scientist who emigrated to England during the Nazi years and a student of the economic structure of the National Socialist Reich, was also doubtful about any attempt to classify the Nazi economy.

> We must recognize once and for all that the structure of the National Socialist economic system does not follow any blueprint, is not based on any consistent doctrine, be it neo-mercantilism, any guild or 'Estate' theory, or liberal or socialist dogma. The organization of the economic system is pragmatic. It is directed entirely by the need of the highest possible efficiency and productivity.[146]

In the Nazi economy man was the only source of value. The better the selection, the greater the value, which in turn lay in more capital in the form of creative spirit and will toward economic work. The new capital of the Nazi Reich was what Nietzsche called the "Capital of intelligence and will", so the Nazi doctrine rejected any economic theory that put economic successes and failures in factors external to the human will. For Hitler, economic success was based primarily on ability and this was a derivative of fertility and selection.

> I do not intend to create a National Socialist economic theory. The only dogma I admit in economic matters is that there is no theory in this field, but knowledge. There are fundamental principles, very concrete and simple, and these are not my property alone but shared by many intelligent men who have been true to themselves and have seen things from a sensible and natural point of view. Economics is only a means to make life easier for men. If someone comes to me saying that he has a wonderful economic theory, I ask him what benefits it has, since I'm not interested in theories but their benefits. If the will to work, performance and intelligence gave way, it would be the end of us. The others formulate theories, we are

---

146 Franz Neumann. *Behemoth, The Structure and Practice of National Socialism.*

working in giant factories and many more are blooming. This is National Socialist economic policy, not theory. These are simple principles, applicable to private life, to society, economy and nature, a natural knowledge, knowledge of the *Life-Laws*. This is the National Socialist economic theory.[147]

For National Socialism, a healthy and abundant economy had to have as its base, or foundation, the qualitative aspects that selection preserved in superior individuals. Thus was born the theory of the "Labor Standard" of National Socialism. Neumann put it with admirable simplicity.

> If gold constitutes wealth, then Germany is indeed poor. But National Socialism insists that gold is not wealth, that all wealth derives from the productivity of man. If that is so, then Germany is the richest country in the world.[148]

For National Socialism, the economic crisis experienced by Germany prior to Nazism was essentially the product of a crisis of valuable men, a crisis produced by decades of counter-selective processes that finally attacked the "Capital of intelligence and will." Recovering that capital was seen by National Socialism as the key to the new economy. In that sense, the control of labor organization was very important for the Reich. The German Labor Front (DAF), Strength Through Joy, After-Work Activity and other institutions that controlled the labor force, also controlled the origin and engine of the new economy. Rather than nationalizing the means of production, National Socialism somehow Nazified the will to work, and with that it became the owner of the new capital.

The economic recovery of the Reich was based on the creation of this new form of capital. It was the State that renewed the will to work through the implementation of large projects that mobilized contractors and workers. The creation of work as a product of State

---

147 Hitler. *Construction Workers Speech*, 1937
148 Franz Neumann. *Behemoth, The Structure and Practice of National Socialism*

investment through unsubsidized bonds was a direct challenge to the international financial system. Hitler created a trillion *reichmarks* without further backing with the "debt-free money" system, issuing "Treasury Certificates of Labor." Hans Kerhl, *SS-Brigadeführer* attached to the "SS Main Office" and responsible for economic issues, clarified that this did not involve the indiscriminate issuance of currency, an error into which desperate economies tended to fall. Sovereign bonds served only to spark the economy by financing large fiscal works. The money without backing in circulation was later withdrawn through the collection of taxes, leaving the economy with a real and organic circulation toward economic growth. *"The banknote machine was not used for financing. The money in circulation from 1932 to 39 increased almost 100%, with a growth in economic activity of not less than 100%"*[149]

The creation of the new Nazi economic capital immediately collided with the capitalist system, especially with one of its most characteristic tools, credit with interest. Ending credit with interest was a key part of the early drafts of the newly founded NSDAP. The party's ideologue, Gottfried Feder, proposed "breaking the slavery of interest". Otto Nathan commented on this point by emphasizing the ideological rather than economic motivation in limiting interest in credit.

> The Nazi government has been very anxious throughout the years of its regime to reduce the interest rates of the various types of loans and bonds; this was partly done for ideological and political reasons. This was admitted by official Nazi sources, who claim that the reduction of interest is not due to fear of the volume of credit, but to the programmatic demonstration of the fundamental attitude toward the credit problem.[150]

But interest-free credit was only the first stage of an economy that sought to eliminate credit as a form of capital altogether. Because interest-free credit remained, after all, credit, it perpetuated the logic that financial

---
[149] Hans Kerhl. *Crisis Manager in the Third Reich*
[150] Otto Nathan. *Nazi War Finance and Banking*

capital created work, and not the "Capital of intelligence and will." The objective of National Socialism was, therefore, to dispense with the credit market, with or without interest, as a way of financing investment and the expansion of the economy. In Nazi ideology it was work that had to create capital, not the other way around.

The consequence of the elimination of credit meant the decline of German banks. During the Nazi Reich the majority of investment was done with private or mutual savings, with the product of work done, and not of work to-be-done.

> The system of savings and mutual banking, with its national roots, was quickly adapted to the National Socialist State. Private banking was generally suspected of being anti-Party, since the NSDAP felt itself absolutely and unequivocally anti-capitalist. The banking world had no influence on the economy, and less on economic policy.[151]

Thanks to the flourishing economic recovery, the government's efforts were able to stimulate saving as a source of capital deposit available for investment and the purchase of private goods. Adam Tooze, a British historian at Yale and Cambridge Universities, even ties the enormous cost of war to this very principle.

> Salaries experienced a sharp rise that led to a massive growth of deposits in savings accounts. Savings were a reason for the flourishing industry in the Third Reich, as well as the source of war financing... As of the autumn of 1938 the Reichsbank banned all new mortgage borrowings... Therefore private investors were left without a financial market in which to speculate, so investments had to be made either in the real economy or by investing in the only form of speculation left during the Third Reich, buying government debt... In addition, borrowing from savers provided a crucial source of tax relief.[152]

---
151 Hans Kerhl. *Crisis Manager in the Third Reich*
152 Adam Tooze. *The Wages of Destruction*

Fertility Law

On the other hand, the Nazi government restricted the capital market as a form of corporate capitalization, and promoted limited companies over anonymous and joint-stock companies.

> The social ideology of National Socialism attacked companies for their actions and their anonymous character. Stock financing is no longer necessary when self-financing has reached such proportions that the attraction of capital market capitalization is nil.[153]

The change in the system of capitalization was directly detrimental to the role of banks, the stock market and the laws of finance capital. Tooze states that the new economy, based on the *Life-Laws* and the Nazi Worldview, had as one of its main consequences the decline of the finance capitalist economy. *"The victory of domestic financing over bank lending pointed to the decline of financial capitalism".*[154] Tooze noted the same effect of the new Nazi economy.

> The Berlin Great Banks were amongst the chief 'losers' of the Nazi economic recovery. Between 1932 and 1939, in which period German output more than doubled, the total assets of the Berlin Great Banks rose by only 15 per cent. By contrast, the assets of the savings banks, the main vehicle for 'popular liquidity', rose by 102 per cent over the same period... The funds accumulating in the accounts of bankers' industrial clients made them more independent than ever before of bank loans.... It is in fact hard to think of any other period in modern German history in which banking institutions had less influence than the period between 1933 and 1945.[155]

---

153 Otto Nathan. *Nazi War Finance and Banking*
154 Adam Tooze. *The Wages of Destruction*
155 Adam Tooze. *The Wages of Destruction*

Economic Biology

Capitalism was from the National Socialist perspective as counter-selective as Marxism, but financial capitalism was more dangerous, since while Marxism was a hypothetical threat, the former had been on German soil for decades. For the Nazi ideology, the capitalist economy tended to produce internal fragmentation and an unnatural individualist struggle, a principle that was not confirmed by nature and its laws. For the Nazi biologist Konrad Lorenz, species did not specialize by competing internally. The groups of organisms that were oriented to internal competition in the so-called "intra-species selection" ended up neglecting the threats of the environment and the other competing groups. The first enemy of a species was another equivalent species on the natural scale, the competitor for the same natural resources. In a second order of things, a group of organisms confronted their predators and, to a lesser extent, their prey. For Lorenz, although species were inwardly confronted with territorial and reproductive competition, this was limited, and selection did not work toward specialization in internal struggle methods. The few natural examples of intra-specific selection resulted in physiological deformity and eventual extinction.

It is for this reason that the fragmented and inorganic action of capitalist entrepreneurship was the first obstacle to the plan of economic renewal based on natural laws. And while private initiative remained an economic engine, that sector's freedom of action of was under tight State control.

> It must be put quite drastically. With Hitler's seizure of power, the great industrialists saw the demise, without compensation, of their former privileged position of media and political influence. They were no longer able to influence the press, and found no friends in government. The NSDAP was true to its anti-capitalist roots. All this must be said clearly.[156]

Hitler was hard on businessmen and industrialists. He threatened

---
156 Hans Kehrl. *Crisis Manager in the Third Reich*

Fertility Law

them with expropriations and even issued an economic boycott law punishable by death. Tooze reports the resolve of *Reichsmarschall* Göring, director of the industrial transformation plan called the *Four Year Plan*, when it came to imposing State objectives.

> Representatives of the six leading steel firms were summoned to a private meeting... Göring had not come to ask for favors... Hitler had given them four years, and they had wasted that time... Göring had lost patience. His job was 'to throw down the saboteurs of rearmament and the *Four Year Plan* and to send them where they belonged [to hell]'... All private holdings of German iron ore deposits would be merged into a single state company... The shocked industrialists were then each handed a map showing the ore fields of their firms that were to be expropriated in the name of the Reichswerke. Göring then read out a decree personally approved by Hitler, which authorized the forced sale.[157]

But, despite threats of expropriation, for Hitler the machines themselves were of no great value. This value was to be found in the "Capital of intelligence and will" and the industrial elite, as good entrepreneurs, certainly had that. The National Socialist government could not dispense with the experience and genius of the big industrialists if it wanted to immediately begin with their plan to separate from the capitalist economy. Taking away factories from the Krupps, who for generations had led steel production, or handing over to State bureaucrats the workshops of Dr. Porsche, where for decades he had led the field in engineering innovation, would be very stupid in the eyes of National Socialism. Hitler was very clear about the uselessness of nationalizing the means of production, the State engaging in commercial work, and overburdening the State with bureaucracy and controls.

For Nazism, businessmen and industrialists had to be re-educated in order to extirpate the tendency towards capitalism and orient them to

---

[157] Adam Tooze. *The Wages of Destruction*

an organic economy based on the *Life-Laws*.

> It is not the government's job to merge the mind with the method of production. Either we have a private industry that does it, or the government has to. In that case we will not need the private sector any more. The role of the minister of economics is to set goals. The private sector must comply. Either industrialists will meet these goals or they will be unable to survive in this modern economy. But in that case it will not be Germany that goes down, but, at the most, a few industrialists.[158]

MONUMENTALITY

The Nazi economy was based on the implementation, without much dogma, of technical tools according to the economic situation at any given time. And while this prevented the creation of a Nazi economic theory, National Socialism built a stable and successful system.

The new economic structure was divided into two areas. The means of production, almost entirely private, were grouped in semi-guilds of private character that in practice were completely controlled by the State. These were the "Circles", organizations under the direction of "General Secretaries" (*Generalbevollmachtig*). The most important general secretaries were: Dillgard for electricity, Schell for motor vehicles, Todt for construction, Lange for the means of production, and Hannecken for iron and steel. General Secretaries made plans and set goals, and "Circles" ran whatever way they thought best. A second organization, the "National Agencies" (*Reichstellen*), also organized by industry, disposed of and distributed the raw materials necessary for production.

Industries and companies were therefore forced to cartelize in order to centralize objectives and combine efforts. The cartelization process started early. In 1933 the first decree was issued to regulate companies

---

[158] Hitler quoted by Neumann. *Behemoth, The Structure and Practice of National Socialism*

that sold commodities and services at prices that made sustainable development impossible. The completion of the compulsory cartelization process meant the creation of the world's largest cartel system. By 1942, the Reich had the incredible number of only 350,000 companies for a population of over 70 million. The stability of the markets through coordinated "cartels" and economic management also allowed the elimination of destructive or "intra-specific" competition and free-market cannibalization.

Quickly the "Cartels" achieved an exponential power of production. A powerful State and NSDAP political power regulated and directed their actions through the "Circles" and "National Agencies": limiting profits, demanding reinvestment and research and conveying the enormous amounts of taxes collected toward social works. The "Cartels" were coordinated and operating within heavily regulated markets, so there was a free and constant transfer of new technologies and patents. For Neumann the "Cartels" undoubtedly produced the expansion of the German economy: *"Cartels have indeed become the organs for attaining full employment with the collaboration and under the pressure of the state."*

The "Combines", another key part of the Nazi economy, were companies from different areas which were forced to coordinate, industrially and commercially, to achieve maximum rationality and efficiency in production and commercial processes. The "Combines" allowed industries of different types to unite in coordinated systems that thereby enhanced production, allowing the creation of products in a coordinated and efficient way. "Circles", "Cartels" and "Combines" allowed for national unity towards objectives like the system of "Community Financing".

"Germany has developed new methods of financing the new technological processes... the so-called 'community financing.'... The financing of the lignite hydrogenation industry is even more striking. The capital requirements are immense and only the wealthy dye trust could take the risk of constructing such a plant. By a decree of 28 September 1934, therefore, a 'compulsory community of the lignite

industry'[cartel] was created... *composed of all lignite mines with a yearly production of 400,000 tons or more.* The community then set up a joint stock corporation for the production of synthetic gasoline from lignite,(*Braun-kohlen-Benzin*)."[159]

During the war years the union of "Circles", "Cartels" and "Combines" was into great economic units was decreed, which definitively erased discrepancies of operation and coordination between the private sector and the State. The "Cartels" and "Combines" which had totaled about 2,300 at the start of the war were compressed and merged, joining with the entire German economy in only 500 public/private conglomerates called *"Reichsvereinigung"*. The most important were the "National Coal Association", the "National Iron Association", and smaller associations dealing with synthetic fibers, textiles, hemp and the shoe industry, among others. The leadership of all the "National Associations" was centralized in the so-called "Central Planning Office" (*Zentralen Planung*), a committee led by State officials, Party, SS and civilian individuals.

THE DANGER OF MONUMENTALITY

Economic monumentality, rising wages, full employment, and especially increased production, produced levels of economic dynamism never before experienced in Germany. The gross domestic product grew steadily during the Nazi period, as did industrial production. For the first time industrial production supplanted artisan industry due to the great masses that were turning for the first time toward the consumption of goods and services. But a highly centralized economy, large factories and production lines, vacations and mass-produced food, among other characteristics of industrialized economies, could overshadow the individual and weaken his "Capital of intelligence and will". For National Socialism, the titanic monumentality of industrial overproduction concealed a threat of crushing the individual and his inventive spirit, transforming all that economic monumentality into a counter-selective process. The huge

---

[159] Franz Neumann. *Behemoth, the Structure and Practice of National Socialism*

industrial cartels and their millions of workers could become lost in what Nietzsche called impersonal slavery.

These were new problems; the Reich had recently initiated a process of accelerated industrialization through the "Four Year Plan" in order to counter the economic siege by other European powers. The plan was based on import substitution through the development of synthetics and maximum efficiency in the exploitation of natural resources. With mass consumption, this process became more acute and, with the coming of war, maximum industrialization was presented as inevitable if the Reich wanted to defeat the combined war effort of the most industrialized countries of the world. Even before the war, the National Socialist economy was undergoing a process of moderate industrialization. The Reich was not equal to The United States, the Soviet Union, England or even France or Belgium, in terms of levels of industrialization. Industry, especially the war material industry, had to initiate very large transformative processes in order to support the necessary production.

Albert Speer, a young architect who became an arms minister, began a process of transforming the war industry along the American model, an industrial process National Socialists sarcastically called "mammoth industry". Speer's nomination was surprising. The new minister had shown organizational skills in urban planning, but apart from that he was far removed from circles familiar with the NS Worldview.

Faced with Speer's American approach to productive work, the SS was alarmed to detect the potential danger of individual depersonalization and the dimming of the inventive genius, a characteristic process of capitalist industrial society. The industrialization that the Reich needed to confront the war and satisfy the high purchasing power of the population was a source of great debate between the proponents of the Worldview and those circles that did not know of the *Life-Laws*. In the struggle for the hegemony of the NS Worldview, the economy was practically the last counter-selective bastion, a redoubt conquered by the SS only months before the end of the war.

This process that brought SS control of the economy was a slow one. National Socialism did not arise out of either the financial-economic sphere or the industrialist class, so its first steps in economic management were more directed to getting control of the economy rather than to its day to day operation. However, in the course of the war the SS became the organization with the greatest economic power in the Reich. The SS was persistent and patient; little by little Himmler managed to infiltrate the different ministries and staff them with his officers, while on the other hand strengthening the SS industrial empire by buying companies and industries. SS Generals Otto Ohlendorf, Franz Hayler, Georg Keppler, Hans Kerhl, and Hans Kammler, among others, occupied key positions in economic management. The concern of the SS was to avoid creating a generation of standardized automatons, so-called mass men (*Massmenschen*), during the transition to a mass consumer economy and industrial-scale production. The exaltation of individual inventiveness, concern for detail, quality production, and all that went into distinguishing superiorly performing individuals (*Leistungmenschen*) was exalted by the SS economic ideology.

The challenge of creating a high-performance man was not looked at in an abstract and theoretical way, but demanded great efforts from intellectuals like SS General Otto Ohlendorf, an adviser to the Ministry of Economics. They had to combine the monumentality and overproduction of a giant industrial power with the National Socialist ideology. Once appointed as senior economic director, Ohlendorf went to work developing a plan to repair the damage done by Speer's mammoth economy. The Ohlendorf plan, called the "Economic Management Reform Plan" and its journal ,the "Economic Policy Review" (*Wirtschafspolitische Bilanze*) criticized Speer's Americanized industrial economy by establishing an entire economic plan based on the NS Worldview as its replacement. Ohlendorf, on behalf of the SS and the Nazi Worldview, showed himself to be a great visionary. He understood the challenges of a modern economy, that the craft era had died forever and that and the great battle for markets was to come. A romantic and artisanal economy, perhaps dreamt of by Nietzsche, had no place in modernity and the Nazi Reich would not shirk from the new industrial horizons. Reforming industrialization, concentrating on qualitative and selective aspects, seemed to be the objective that the SS intended to meet throughout the surprising process of intense industrialization required to fight the world war.

1944 was marked by Hitler's complete distrust both of Speer and of the production of weapons in a technical-industrial Americanized way. Although the first stage of industrialization was relatively successful, centralized organization in particular, the expected growth was never fully realized and the quality of military articles and equipment fell to a level unthinkable by German standards. This caught the attention of the SS, which began moving in an economic direction. With control of the key ministries, Himmler managed to get hold of important industrial conglomerates that formed the pillar of his brief but gigantic empire. Soon the SS was the main producer of armaments and a major producer of non-war-related consumer goods. The SS was involved in the mining of magnesium, quartz and semi-precious stones, and even in oil extraction.

In the last months of war the SS controlled all the ministries of the Reich. Himmler had achieved his purpose; the Reich's industry was, briefly, run according to the NS Worldview. Not only had financial capitalism been eliminated from economic life, but industrialization, a process closely linked to capitalist accumulation, had radically changed focus. The Nazi Worldview managed to dominate, for a few months, the last area of the Reich where it had not previously achieved absolute mastery of the economy. If the Reich had won the war, it would most likely have become an SS State.

In the postwar period Speer came to recognize that the SS's analysis had shown remarkable prescience regarding the economic and even anthropological problems of mass society born of industrial overproduction during World War II. Decades after the end of the war, still afraid of recognizing the assertiveness of the Nazi Worldview, Speer never stopped thinking about the concerns raised by Hitler's and the SS's ideas.

Ohlendorf began the transition of the basic concepts of the

economy into the postwar period. His plan had to do with nebulous National Socialist economic ideas. In 1932 Hitler said that industrialization had enslaved man and had tied him to capital by totally destroying him, and that only Nazi socialism would restore the person to his individual sphere by restoring development as a service to man. These theories had declined since I successfully introduced Americanism into the organization of arms production. But in 1944 Ohlendorf, certainly one of the most brilliant National Socialist intellectuals, put before the economic council of the Party: "We must question any economic structure on the basis of whether it fosters the development of Germanic characteristics. We must make very sure that we can realize the elements of our Worldview economically. The goods we produce in the postwar period are not essential, but rather in order to preserve and develop the substance of our biological values". This goal, Ohlendorf said, was threatened by my production principles. Ohlendorf continues: "If we can introduce our Worldview even in the economic administration area, we can finally achieve an order that allows the development of human strength together with man's divine mission".

Ohlendorf planned a European economic order that contrasted with capitalism and Bolshevism, systems that did not allow self-responsibility or the development of economic activity. Ohlendorf wondered if this war with its mass production of armaments had not thrown us into a new era, if we were not at the beginning of a new industrial era that would remain after the war, and if so, how would the industry tresfer this knowledge to the popular industry, for example, clothes or food production, since obviously wartime production would be transferred to the postwar period.

Ohlendorf wondered: "Can Europe compete with North America or Asia in mass production? If competition among monumental producers begins, and if this competition becomes fundamental to the Reich, we must ensure that we win this competition, but

Fertility Law

we must safeguard the individual in his personal sphere and his happiness".

No matter what comes out of this war, if we must compete with North America or Japan we must confront the massive with the qualitative. The strength of the people lies in preserving and expanding qualitative skills'. Ohlendorf doubted even if the path of industrialization could be fully traversed. "Where will we get food for all those masses that will live in the city? What will happen when the field is emptied due to industrialization? We will end up with an undesirable massification in industry, collective entertainment and recreation. If we use technology as an end in itself, as the foundation of development, then the *Life-Laws* will have no alternative but to subordinate themselves to technological organization. Economics would then not be determined by human development and progress, but by rigid thinking and rational method".

Hitler's influence can be read word-by-word in the ideology of Ohlendorf, his notions were taken from the ideological substance of National Socialism. Many things that Ohlendorf proclaimed were premonitory to current problems. Today I adhere to similar demands, but I have doubts when I discover the parallels between his thinking then and mine now. The concern I feel for the individual still goes back to the words of Ohlendorf.[160]

---

160 Adapted from Albert Speer. *Infiltration: How Heinrich Himmler Schemed to Build an SS Industrial Empire*

Heredity Law

For National Socialism, the selection law and the fertility law were based on the transmission of heritable characteristics. The law governing this transmission was the *Law of Inheritance* (Gesetz der Vorerbung).

The *Law of Inheritance* was based on the laws of Gregor Mendel and the theory of evolution closest to the research of Ernst Haeckel. Mendel's basic rules — published in the middle of the nineteenth century but forgotten until their rediscovery in the early twentieth century— were the foundation of genetics. Before the rediscovery of these laws, inheritance was only vaguely understood, Darwin himself thought that the organs secreted through the blood certain hereditary factors that at the moment of conception were fused together in a single fluid. This theory was to change at the beginning of the 20th century when Hugo de Vries, Carl Correns and the Austrian Erich von Tschermak, all of whom would later work closely with the NSDAP, and especially with SS General Walther Darré. They speculated on the existence of microscopic physical units, the so-called genes, to explain the laws of genetic inheritance.

For National Socialism, the laws of inheritance would allow procreation to be directed towards the goals of evolutionary improvement. Recovering and expanding this scientific knowledge to spread it to the entire population was very important in the Nazi struggle for biological-evolutionary revitalization. Knowledge about inheritance had to transcend the narrow scope of the laboratories and make its way into the broader society to counteract harmful counter-selective effects. To this end, educational campaigns to disseminate the inheritance law were established, and there was wide promotion of biologically-minded doctrinal instruction in all Movement organizations. This cultural diffusion was called the "Victory of of life-law thinking" (*Sieg des Lebensgesetzlichen denken*).

In 1938, evolution and Mendelian theories were compulsory subjects in all study and training centers. At that time the Minister of Education stated that "students should accept and study something as obvious, essential and important as the natural law of the elimination of the less adapted together with the evolution and the emergence of races in connection with animal evolution" [Cited by Weikart]. Evolution, inheritance laws and Mendel's laws were also widely disseminated by official bodies such as the NSDAP journal *The People's Observer* (Völkischer Beobachter), as well as the *National Socialist Monthly Bulletin* (Nationalsozialistische Monatshefte) edited by Rosenberg; the magazine *Will and Power* (Wille und Macht); the publication *People and Race* (Volk und Rasse) of the SS Race and Settlements Main Office, edited by the education body of the NSDAP.

The instruction manuals of the NS Worldview, sent to SS troops coming from all social backgrounds and levels of education, strove to explain genetic inheritance and its relation to propensity for disease, physiological degeneration and all kinds of counter-selective factors. The implications of heredity, fertility, correct mate selection (Gattenwahl), the relationship with the environment (Umwelt), and Living Space (Lebensraum) were all concepts that were successfully inserted into the cultural life of the Reich at a time when these things were unknown to the general population.

> The scientific understanding of the importance of blood for the existence of the German people and their culture did not succeed in imposing itself without putting up the necessary fight. Our people's thinking had been deceived. Only the National Socialist Worldview allowed the people to think racially. When National Socialism took power, most citizens did not understand the revolutionary importance of science and genetics. The triumph of racial thought in such a short time was impressive. Scientific knowledge generally takes decades, even centuries to get into popular thinking. The Worldview Adolf Hitler has developed, based on incontrovertible scientific results, has allowed people

to be persuaded of the importance of racial thought. And the peoples of Europe too, especially our allies, already recognize the importance of racial thought. Examples are Slovakia, Romania, Hungary and Croatia. The manifesto of the scientists of Fascist Italy clearly affirms racial thought.[161]

HEREDITY SCIENCE

In the Nazi Worldview the *Law of Inheritance* was a natural law that determined the value of an individual. In this sense, international science also endorsed the importance of inheritance, but it was given less importance as a determining factor in man's intellectual and volitional characteristics, which were attributed rather to cultural, educational, nutritional or even metaphysical processes. The real challenge of the Nazi Worldview was to strengthen the idea that these spiritual characteristics were also transferred through biological inheritance, and to establish the importance of developing a modern science and public policies aimed at physical and intellectual improvement.

> Our every look at the world confirms that the offspring resemble their ancestors. Inheritance is an ancient knowledge of mankind. Breeders have always tried to promote the transferal of certain characteristics and to prevent others in animals and plants. That this is a form of development according to natural laws has nevertheless been recognized and tested only over the last few decades. The *Law of Inheritance*, like the other *Life-Laws*, has the same validity for plants, animals and humans. Inheritance is therefore the transfer of characteristics from parents to offspring. And not only are the physical characteristics transferred, but so are the intellectual and psychological.[162]

Insofar as inheritance was the law that determined physical as well as the intellectual characteristics, the study and knowledge of inheritance played a part in communal progress and even the survival of the people.

---

161 SS-Hauptamt. *Racial Policy*
162 SS-Hauptamt. *SS Mate Selection and Race*

National Socialism - Its Principles and Philosophy

Knowing the laws of inheritance had to be part of the Reich's culture and its scientific research could not fall into ideological speculations. That is why, contrary to certain postwar speculations, a review of the Nazi instruction manuals shows the scientific rigor with which the subject of genetic inheritance was diffused. Ute Deichmann, an expert in the development of professional biology, endorses this fact.

> We must note that during the Nazi period the study of human evolution was by no means suppressed or influenced from above along specific ideological paths. At no time was there a National Socialist view of biology with a uniform ideology. The work of biologists remained within the parameters of the scientific method. The theory of a National Socialist created and oriented biology, is false. There were many prominent biologists working in this field such as Ludwig von Bertalanffy and his contribution to organism (later known worldwide as General Systems Theory), botanist Ernst Lehmann, zoologist and later Nobel Prize winner Konrad Lorenz, who joined the NSDAP and the Bureau of Racial Policy, and Gerhard Heberer, an internationally renowned zoologist and anthropologist.[163]

The Nazi Worldview moved early to investigate and disseminate the *Law of Inheritance* in a scientific tone. Its ideological instruction manuals resembled actual biology classes more than political texts. In these instructional manuals there were no traces of whimsical ideas or the vociferations of a hysterical racism full of cultural anxieties.

For National Socialism heritable structures were not fixed but plastic, with mutations, or random changes in the genes that renewed the possibilities available to face the ever-changing conditions of struggle. Without this capacity for change allowing for error in genetic copy, heritable structure would be fixed, limiting the number of possibilities when adapting to the environment. Only that heritable structure which was successful in the struggle for life could become an unalterable characteristic, not in danger of elimination by selection. But this

---

163 Ute Deichmann. *Biologists Under Hitler*

fixation was never eternal, since copying errors would shortly need to be tested against ever-changing environmental conditions. Without genetic mutation and subsequent selection, the biological renewal plan of Nazism would make no sense, since regaining genetic traits that were successful under past conditions would not present benefits for future challenges. The genetic plasticity provided by random mutations was a key element in the possibilities for genetic renewal in the NS Worldview. Heinz Brücher, SS sub-lieutenant (*SS-Untersturmführer*) and one of the most important SS biologists, clearly outlined the plastic nature of the inheritance law in the guidance manuals.

> Nature, like people's lives, is a relentless struggle. Just as with people, where the most gifted, the most intense, the most vigorous, or the best developed is victorious, so it is in the savage life of nature that surrounds us, where only the fittest survive. But the struggle for existence and selection can only be fought with the presence of different base materials. These differences in living things are found in their genes. Hereditary factors are the inner strength of every living being. Hereditary factors are stable, since they maintain specific types, but on the other hand these are not immutable and undergo minor alterations. In order to understand the effect of inheritance, we have to look at a very small structure visible only with a microscope. All living creatures have in their cells a semi-liquid cytoplasm in which we find a nucleus. This is the most important carrier of genetic information. In it, we find the chromosomes, of which each species of living thing has different quantities. Each chromosome has a very interesting, though microscopic, structure. In the chromosomes, hereditary factors or genes are ordered longitudinally. From these arise the mysterious agents which control the hereditary factors of organisms. From minor changes in the construction or in the composition of chromosomes, specific genes can undergo modifications, this is called mutation. Through mutations, specific genes can disappear, new ones can emerge, and complete chromosomes can break or duplicate and modify. Although these mutations occur only in small fractions that are far below one percent of

total offspring, they are there, which allows for the great number of living things we know. These mutations are the inexhaustible source of specialization. Adverse genetic changes are soon eradicated by selection, but valuable mutations are maintained, and selection is made. Mutations in genes and environmental selection are the decisive factors in specialization.[164]

National Socialism understood that the key to inheritance was in the cell nucleus. More than two decades before James Watson and Francis Crick discovered the structure of DNA, Nazi scientists were on the same path. Gerhard Schramm, a pioneer virology geneticist and SS officer, was able to understand the role of nucleic acid in the self-replication of a mosaic virus in tobacco, and could replicate it in the year 1938. Later, he was able to extract ribonucleic acid or RNA and determine its importance in inheritance, as well as to give insight into the structure of the chromosome chain. James Watson, in his book about the discovery of the structure of DNA, the research that won him a Nobel Prize in 1963, highlights Schramm's early contributions to the subject.

> Experiments of the German Gerhard Schramm, first published in 1944, reported that TMV particles in mild alkali fell apart into free RNA and a large number of similar, if not identical, protein molecules. Virtually no one outside Germany, however, thought that Schramm's theory was right. This was because of the war. It was inconceivable to most people that the German beasts would have permitted the extensive experiments underlying his claims to be routinely carried out during the last years of a war they were so badly losing. It was all too easy to imagine that the work had direct Nazi support, or that his experiments were incorrectly analyzed. But when I read Bernal's paper, however, I suddenly became enthusiastic about Schramm...[165]

---

164 Heinz Brücher. Inheritance and Breeding. *Guidance Notebooks*, SS-Hauptamt
165 James Watson. *The Double Helix*

Mate Selection

In the Nazi genetic consensus, each biological trait was controlled by two hereditary factors. This pair of factors came from the inheritance of each parent and was located parallel to a specific place on the chromosome. Groups of these pairs formed genes, molecules that directed biological processes that eventually led to physiological characteristics and organic functions. According to the Nazi *Law of Inheritance*, when each heritable factor was equal to its other half, both delivered the same genetic information, determining the characteristic without conflict. This was common in determining the species' generic characteristics. But as to the more specific characteristics of the human species, existing genetic variety triggered conflicts to determine which controlled the organic characteristic. Thus only one factor was determinant and another was recessive. The determining factor controlled the characteristic by expressing its genetic information. The recessive factor was either deactivated or silenced but unaltered and transferable to a new generation to deliver its genetic information when that aligned with another recessive factor present in a new union. The sum of determining factors, expressed in physical and mental appearance, was called "phenotype". The sum of inheritable determinants and recessive factors was called "genotype" or total heritable structure. The genotype could carry across generations recessive traits to suddenly align with other recessive traits emerging as part of an individual's phenotype. That is why for Nazism a mere external evaluation was not conclusive in the knowledge of the genetic value of an individual. Only the knowledge of the laws of inheritance and the correct choice of couple (*Gattenwahl*), through the knowledge of the familiar biological history, served to enhance characteristics oriented to the evolutionary improvement and the victory in struggle for the existence.

> Man has two hereditary factors. The child receives these factors in equal parts from their parents. Offspring with non-equivalent genetic mix may have the appearance of pure offspring as a result of the transfer of predominant hereditary factors into their physical appearance. But the non-expressed heritable factors are not eliminated, they simply did not manifest in that generation.

An external evaluation can therefore never be conclusive. If it were only physical differences that separate human races, the question of belonging to a race would be of little importance. Therefore the appearance of man must be strictly left aside. The hereditary constitution of a person has a far greater meaning than that of appearance. At their crossing these hereditary factors are randomly aligned, resulting in offspring diverse in their heritable composition. The *Law of Inheritance* now forms the basis of knowledge, formation and development of future generations. From the fact that healthy and diseased hereditary factors are both passed on to offspring, knowledge of inheritance and the responsibility to intervene and improve, restrict and promote, for the proper formation of future generations, is of enormous importance. At the time of conception, the essence and worth of a person as regards the well-being of his people and his race are already determined. The correct choice of partner is not only a prerequisite to the preservation of the species, but also for the continuation of a high-value selection.[166]

The heredity law of the Nazi Worldview was certainly deterministic, but it also gave the environment an important place in forming the personality. For National Socialism, factors such as food, climate and education produced biological effects on physical and intellectual characteristics, but the key to the *Law of Inheritance* was in understanding that these factors were not themselves heritable.

In the course of life only a fraction of heritable traits are manifested. Each person has a large treasury of hereditary factors. The environment has its part in the formation of individuals, but does not alter heritable characteristics. The preservation of Germaneness in various different soils on the planet is a testament to the strength of blood. Certainly, education and the environment can develop and promote some traits and restrict others, but the fundamental essence remains unchanged. Appearance is subject to many changes due to environment, but not the hereditary

---

166 SS-Hauptamt. *SS Mate Selection and Race*

structure behind it. Acquired skills are not heritable. Only through selection are the heritable characteristics transmitted. Marxists and Democrats have tried, very imaginatively, to prove that the environment can improve the destiny of peoples.[167]

In the eyes of Nazism, policies aimed at creating heritable genetic value were more durable and fundamental than policies aimed at improvement based on non-heritable factors. Physical development through sport and healthy eating, or the accumulation of intellectual knowledge through rigorous education were not characteristics capable of perpetuating themselves in a community, since they were not capacities transferable by genetic inheritance. Genetics was, in the eyes of Nazism, the basis for cultural development and the progress of peoples. On this basis it was possible to structure lasting and effective health and education policies.

EVOLUTIONIST SYNTHESIS

The close link between the Worldview and the biological sciences was central to National Socialism. The SS developed a highly scientific view of the *Life Laws* that went hand in hand with a process toward hegemony over academic research. Slowly, the SS was incorporating scientists into their ranks and preparing their cadres with solid knowledge of biology and genetics.

Nazi genetic science had one of its greatest representatives in the doctor and SS Brigadier (*SS-Oberführer*) Rudolf Mentzel. He joined the "Council of Natural Sciences" in the Ministry of Education as a biologist. He was also appointed director of the "German Research Association", the main funding body for biological research in the Reich. Mentzel led all research on genetics and biology during the war, in conjunction with SS Brigadier Konrad Meyer. At the same time, the SS created a genetic research institute called Alt-Rehse, whose director was the doctor and SS Officer Hermann Böhm. Himmler also ordered the SS to take control of the prestigious University of Jena to turn it into a center of SS biological studies.

---

167 SS-Hauptamt. *Believe and Fight*

The mission of running a university under the auspices of the Worldview was entrusted to SS Colonel (*SS-Standartenführer*) Karl Astel, anthropologist and leader of the Reich's anti-tobacco crusade. Astel was appointed rector of the University in 1939, and in that capacity he appointed other SS officers to the key rectories. Thus it was that biologist and SS Sub-lieutenant (*SS-Untersturmführer*) Heinz Brücher, zoologist and SS Sub-lieutenant Gerhard Heberer, SS Major (*SS-Sturmbannführer*) Johann von Leers and doctor and SS Captain (*SS-Hauptamt*) Lothar Stengel-von Rutkowski came together to form the SS vanguard at the ancient university. These officers represented the Nazi Worldview within the field of genetic and biological research and their mission was to create a university under the parameters of a modern biological science.

Richard Weikart, in his article "The Role of Darwinism in Nazi Racial Thought," states that it is enough to read some of the doctrinal material, and even the magazines and newspapers of the time, to immediately notice the evolutionary, scientific aura of Nazi ideology. For Weikart Nazi thought contained several points in line with the scientific rigor of the time.

> First, the belief that humans evolved from primates. Second, an evolutionary explanation for the development of different races, including the Nordic or Aryan. Specifically, they believed that the Nordic race became the superior race due to the difficult climatic conditions of the northern European Ice Age, defined by a struggle for existence which caused the weak to perish, leaving only the most vigorous. Third, that differentiated evolutionary development provided the scientific evidence of racial inequality. Fourth, racial inequality was cloistered within an inevitable struggle for existence. Fifth, that the way for one's own race to triumph in this struggle was to procreate more prolifically than the other competing races and to gain more living space. Sixth, many believed that this Darwinism promoted a collectivist ideal.[168]

---

168 Richard Weikart. *The Role of Darwinism in Nazi Racial Thought*

This scientific vision allowed the SS to become involved in the academic production of important biological research material. In 1940, scientists sponsored by the SS published "Foundations of the Hereditary Biology of Man" (Die Grundlagen der Erbbiologie des Menschen), where human heredity research was integrated with the new science of molecular biology. One of the main editors was SS officer Gerhard Heberer. For Ute Deichmann;

> Heberer was and is considered as one of the leading scientists in the field of evolutionary engineering, especially in the human area. Heberer promoted the idea of evolution with missionary zeal, and as a member of the SS he fought against the attacks directed against Haeckel and the theory of human evolution. Heberer received support from the SS Office of Race and Health.[169]

In his work, Heberer was explicit about the new orientation of racial science and insisted on perspectives of the physiological future that would allow for the containment of biological counter-selection, to such an extent that he went beyond the conservative views on race and genetics. He criticized;

> Those in the humanities who saw the theory of evolution as 'naive' and with an inappropriate sense of certainty merely showed how out of touch they were with the importance of the theory for an understanding of the world and the formulation of a clear understanding of reality. This was also true of a 'completely chaotic' literature which... typically led to an unbridled mysticism.[170]

In 1942 Heberer, with the patronage of the SS, acted as editor of the important publication "Evolution of Organisms" (*Die Evolution der Organismen*), a text that synthesized all the evolutionary knowledge of the National Socialist Reich. Thomas Junker and Uwe Hossfeld

---

169 Ute Deichmann. *Biologists Under Hitler*
170 Hutton, paraphrasing Heberer

in their revealing article "The Architects of Evolutionary Synthesis in National Socialist Germany," note the importance of this publication in the history of Western evolutionary synthesis. For Junker and Hossfeld, the contribution of Nazi scientists to the global evolutionary synthesis was fundamental, but at the same time largely unknown. Of the scientists who promoted the "Evolutionary Synthesis" in Germany, 70% were members of the NSDAP, 30% of the SS, 25% of the SA, 35% belonged to the "National Socialist League of University Teachers" and 65% to "The National Socialist League of Teachers". The same research reveals that the sector most committed to evolutionism was centered around the SS. Heberer's collaborators on that fundamental text included the main scientists of the Nazi Reich, men like Hans Bauer, SS officer and member of the Ancestor's Heritage Office (*Ahnenerbe*); Timofeeff-Ressousky; Konrad Lorenz, member of the NSDAP; Christian von Krogh, SS officer and Ahnenerbe member; Wilhelm Gieseler, another SS officer and Ahnenerbe member; Hugo Dingler, SS officer; Hans Weinert, SS officer; and Bernard Rensch, among other anthropologists, geneticists, zoologists and botanists. The work, which saw numerous editions during the post-war period, addressed matters that were very advanced for the time, such as the evolutionary effect of population size, geographic isolation, unknown random mutations, as well as other factors affecting creating heritable characteristics such as migrations, polyploidy, macromutations and others.

Racial Biology

But while the NS Worldview drew from the latest scientific advances to build its ideological foundation, especially those related to genetics and human evolution, this is often mistakenly taken for a kind of social Darwinism. Social Darwinism, the creation of Herbert Spencer, is a liberal interpretation of Darwinian and Lamarckian evolutionist theories. And, if for National Socialism, the *Life-Laws* were oriented towards group biological objectives, for Spencer the struggle for existence was within an individualist utilitarian framework. In social Darwinism, the most adapted individuals reaped economic benefits. To ensure this, in Spencer's envisioned society, the State would refrain from interfering in the personal affairs of citizens, not exerting corrective or subsidiary policies that curb competition and mitigate struggle. Nazi evolutionism, meanwhile, rejected competition at the individual level, the so-called "intra-specific competition" proposed by liberal and conservative schools of thought linked to social Darwinism. Nazism was racially socialist and the State was concerned with leveling social conditions among individual citizens as a means of applying rigorous selection criteria. The Nazi State, exercising its regulatory power, tried to erase what it considered to be the anomalies that capitalism, liberalism, and bourgeois life had introduced into society, to create equal social and economic conditions so that the selection processes would become impartial, without artificial or extra-biological advantages such as money, clubs of political and religious influence, or counter-selective ideologies. Instead of individual material gain, the most adapted in Nazi society were obligated to take on greater responsibilities in the hierarchies of the Reich and to choose biologically suitable mates to form elite eugenic family units (clans). Another difference with the typical evolutionism of the West was the mechanistic character of the latter. The Nazi Worldview was vitalist instead, because it did not explain the universe as a mechanism, leaving the ultimate engine of life a mystery.

The final major difference with Western evolutionary theories, and especially with social Darwinism, was in how the two addressed physiological degeneration within a society. While Darwinism opted for sterilization and genetic alteration as corrective tools in the counter-selective processes, the Nazi Worldview preferred to apply and reinforce the criteria of natural selection by teaching the laws of inheritance via mass education and through mate selection.

While it is true that the Nazi State became involved in eugenic practices, these policies were not based on Hitler's Worldview, but from scientists who were disciples of eugenic theories that largely originated in the United States. The one time Hitler referred to these practices, in more than three years of his compiled *Table Talk* conversations, he was quite unenthusiastic about them:

> I was shown a questionnaire drawn up by the Ministry of the

Interior, which it wished to be put to people deemed desirable to sterilize. At least three-quarters of the questions asked would have defeated my own good mother. One I recall was: 'Why does a ship made of steel float in the water?' If this system had been introduced before my birth, I am pretty sure I should never have been born at all!

Let us, for God's sake, throw open the windows and let the fresh air blow away nonsense of this nature! Put the young men into the Army, whence they will return refreshed and cleansed of eight years of such scholastic slime![171]

The new Nazi genetic synthesis, also called Racial Biology (*Rassenbiologie*), had an evolutionary vision that drew more from the scientific thinking of Ernst Haeckel than of Darwin. Haeckel was a 19th century German naturalist who approached evolutionary biological science from a perspective parallel to Darwinism, but less mechanistic and without the scientific dualism of the Cartesian system. In the Reich, to talk about evolution was to speak of Haeckel and the Worldview largely grounded in his evolutionary vision. The SS scientific vanguard at the University of Jena was dedicated to spreading Haeckel's work and giving it a special place in the scientific world. The SS magazine *Biology* (*Der Biologie*) constantly exalted the German naturalist and vigorously celebrated his centenary. The most determined promoter of the great evolutionary scientist was the aforementioned SS officer and biologist Heinz Brücher, who with SS sponsorship published the first biography of the naturalist. For Ute Deichmann, Ernst Haeckel was the SS's great prophet of genetic science. A group of the foremost SS scientists, which included Astel, Brücher, Heberer, Victor Julius Franz, von Leers, as well as Lothar Stengel-von Rutkowski, were his steadfast promoters and defenders. Daniel Gasman, in his book *The Scientific Foundations of National Socialism,* places special emphasis on Haeckel's influence on the Nazi theory of the inheritance. Gasman presents Hitler, and even Nietzsche, as influenced by the Haeckelian theories and the anti-metaphysical, scientific view of man.

---

171 Hitler. *Table Talk*

Adulation of the supremacy of science, elevated to the level of the philosophical, is found again and again in National Socialism. Even among Nazis who never specifically mentioned Haeckel, the influence of the Haeckelian theory is evident. In Himmler, for example, the biological view greatly influenced his thinking. All National Socialist literature was steeped in the veneration of nature and adherence to the dictates of science. Nazism completely assimilated Haeckel's ideas. In the Table Talk, one of Hitler's most-used words is Wissenschaft, science. From his conversations it is evident that Hitler felt bound to the scientific and rational tradition of Europe. But it was clear to Hitler, as it was to Haeckel, that science did not mean a special application of rational culture, but a correct reading of nature. For Hitler, the meaning of nature was not important, but an understanding of nature was necessary to describe the world as it is, and one must accept its rules. But the reason for these natural laws, or their origin, we will never know.[172]

THE ANCESTOR'S HERITAGE

The new Nazi biologism succeeded in overthrowing a number of myths that kept the initial Racial Policy of National Socialism in real blind alleys. The scientific vision of inheritance was displacing a vision loaded with subjectivity that certain groups entrenched in the Movement were striving to elevate as an ideological foundation. This conflict created serious tensions within the Movement which were especially reflected in the inheritance research centre, called "Ancestors Heritage Office" (*Ahnenerbe*), an entity directed by Herman Wirth, historian and philosopher linked to the mystical world of the German nationalist movement.

Wirth career was full of controversies; the main ones were related to his methodological disorder, which many branded as fanciful and not very rigorous. Wirth's research was geared to the archaeological past and permanently intermingled with legends of dubious origin

---

172 Daniel Gasman. *The Scientific Origins of National Socialism*

which ultimately undermined the scientific objectives of the SS. Bernard Mees in his book *The Science of Swastika*, accounts for the unsustainable situation facing the Office of Ancestral Heritage.

> Himmler noted in a letter dated October 1936 that Wirth suffered from a lack of discipline and tried to reason with him so he would not get into such foolish things. Hitler had attacked the idea of Atlantean Nordicism in the annual congress of the Party the previous month, in addition there was an increase of critics even within the Ahnenerbe. By 1937 the independence of Wirth was reduced, he was appointed honorary president and subsequently marginalized the following year.[173]

The situation of Wirth had bottomed and with him the romantic approach of the Indo-Germanic inheritance.

> Gradually after the fall of Wirth, a radical change of focus was experienced in the early years of the war. Upon being replaced by Walther Wüst, SS officer, intellectual and rector of the University of Munich, a stage of professionalization required by Himmler begins. Gone was an approach to the past involving mysticism and fantasy.[174]

This change in methodological focus involved directing the work of the research centre from the study of historical and cultural heritage to biological and genetic research. An example of the new direction was the expedition to Tibet under the leadership of zoologist and SS Mayor (*SS-Sturmbannführer*) Ernst Schäfer, whose main objective was the collection of seeds for the creation of the SS Institute for Plant Genetics of Lanach Castle, Directed by SS sub-lieutenant SS (*SS-Untersturmführer*) Heinz Brücher, alongside genetic researchers such as SS (*SS-Hauptsturmführer*) Konrad von Rauch. The study of simple seeds and organisms was at that time the best way to do genetic research and all the biologists of the world made efforts to have collections

---

173 Bernard Mees. *The Science of Swastika*
174 Bernard Mees. *The Science of Swastika*

with which to experiment. Brücher and von Rauch traversed Europe in search of samples for genetic research and its application in Racial Policy. In Ukraine, during the war, they got hold of a booty of the largest seeds collection of the world, that of the Soviet researcher Tromfim Lysenko. This was one of the most unknown chapters of the struggle between the Nazi and Soviet Worldview. The State of the Soviets oriented its genetic research under the Lamarckist prism, a scientific mainstream established by Jean-Baptiste Lamarck, based on the hybridization theory of the genes and the evolution of the species through mutations influenced by the environment. For Lysenko — converted by Stalin into an official geneticist of agricultural planning— genes could be "reeducated" through external factors. Soviet genetics, as well as the liberal science of Western Europe, argued that genes could be automated and transformed with the aim of adapting to the environment in a sort of evolutionary self-consciousness that did not need natural selection. Nazi scientists argued instead that this was not possible, since it was the selective processes that determined which genes, born of chance from mutations and not from a biological pseudo-consciousness, were successful in the struggle for existence.

Racial biology based on the Evolutionary Synthesis opened up new possibilities for the policies of regeneration of Nazism. Left behind was a romantic and pseudo-mystic vision of the past and an anthropological science obsessed with fixed physical types and a purported original purity.

> The debate on the racial issue was genetically inclined. Racial anthropology needed to argue that racial types were permanent and could not offer a dynamic and progressive view of the German people. The old racist anthropology with a conservative and nostalgic view did not fit well with the revolutionary and radical eugenic utopia of the new genetics. Academic anthropological alchemy allowed reconstructing proto-languages, ancestral racial types, but these were only paper exercises. No political agenda could come out of this. This became clear in the early years of the regime when this faction of anthropologists was neutralized. Nazism needed to

offer a definition of the progress of the people that allowed to combine the genetic inheritance with the inheritance of acquired characteristics. Racial materialism did not make any allowance for individual or collective will to influence a people's destiny. This racial pessimism had its roots in the theories of Gobineau and Spengler and was to become the intellectual target of Nazi science.

Modern science offered a theoretical framework in which degeneration could be understood and avoided and therefore had an essential role in the progressive view of Nazism based on a racially purified people. This model reconciled scientific universalism with Volkisch's particularity and showed how the supremacy of nature and natural processes can exist in parallel with the demands of cultural domination over the environment, in addition, it complemented determinism with voluntarism, science and ideology, offering a dynamic and vital future for the German people.[175]

THE BODY'S GREAT REASON

But Nazi biological science did more than just widen the prospects for new paths of evolutionary vigor. Nazi biology also implied a break with historic anthropology, since the Nazi *Law of Inheritance* stood at odds with the traditional Western way of understanding human essence.

Since its beginnings, the Western tradition has fragmented man into body, soul, and spirit, a perspective that removes certain human capacities of man from the realm of natural laws. For the West, the body is a kind of container, an entity inferior to the soul and the rationality of the mind. Thus, National Socialism faced-off with all the worldviews that sought the source of the human essence in extra-biological realities.

---

[175] Christopher M. Hutton. *Race and the Third Reich*

Heredity Law

Today we are in the middle of another revolutionary era. The scientific revolutionary understanding of genetics and race has found political expression in the National Socialist Worldview. Again, a world of superficialities collapses, a world that has hidden the true nature of humanity and the relationship of body, soul, and spirit. The foundation of the Christian worldview is the doctrine of body-soul separation,. In this view soul and spirit belong to a world independent of the physical, free of natural bonds and even capable, to some extent, of liberating the human body of its natural composition. The human soul does not exist independently of the body, as the church tries to teach. Body and soul are an inseparable unit. The body is the manifestation of the soul. It is a great achievement that racial theory recognizes this unity of body, soul, and spirit and understands them as a whole that follows the eternal laws of nature. A new epoch is on the horizon, one perhaps more revolutionary than the one birthed by Copernicus' work. Ideas about humanity and Volk that have dominated for millennia are collapsing. Mendel was the first to discover the laws of genetics, opening the way to understand one of God's greatest secrets, nature and the continuation of life. Genetics tells us that traits pass unchanged from generation to generation and that spiritual traits are inherited with physical traits.[176]

Per the *Law of Inheritance*, success was measured as being the extent to which man regained his natural essence. A foundational aspect of the *Law of Inheritance*, and of the laws of the Worldview more generally, was the understanding of Man as a privileged living being, but not dissimilar in substance from all other living beings.

"As with everything in nature, heredity is subject to unchangeable laws. *The Law of Inheritance,* like all *Life-Laws*, is true of plants, animals, and men. And not only physical characteristics are heritable, but psychological and intellectual as well."[177].

---

176 SS-Hauptamt. *Racial Policy*
177 SS-Hauptamt. *SS Mate Selection and Race*

National Socialism - Its Principles and Philosophy

The Worldview was very clear, that the soul and the spirit were evolutionary tools that encompassed wonderful things, and had elevated man above the other creatures of the earth, but even so all of this was controlled by the *Law of Inheritance* like any other biological characteristic. For the Nazi intellectuals, soul and spirit were part of biologism, an inseparable part of human corporeality.

> What is inherited? Everything that constitutes a man on a physical, spiritual, and psychic level.[178]

In the *Law of Inheritance*, the body was seen as an entity of domination, the biological wellspring of the will to survive.

> Like the rest of living beings, man is a part of the Earth's abundant diversity. As a part of nature as a whole, it is subject to the general *Life-Laws*, even though it has a particularism assigned to it by its psycho-spiritual abilities, which elevates it far above plants and animals. But in spite of these great abilities it is wrong to separate it from nature. From the *Life-Laws*, it follows that man is a physical, psychic, and spiritual entity, and only through a harmony of these three forces can man achieve a superior value. Non-biological systems of thought tend to fragment this unity and construct its world either mechanistically or exclusively mentally and spiritually, denying the flesh.[179]

For Alfred Bäumler, the official National Socialist philosopher of biologism, corporeality was a phenomenon far more complex than one might think at first, a phenomenon that encompassed aspects of soul and spirit. What the Western tradition called the body, to Bäumler was an abstraction that reduced the phenomenon of the body to a cold instinctive entity that set aside its psychic and rational aspects. For Bäumler, following the Nietzschean legacy, corporeality was very uniquely human, from which emanated man's feeling of unity and consciousness, his Self.

---

178 Anonymous. Fourth example taken from the Sippenamt. *Guidance Notebooks*, SS-Hauptamt
179 SS-Hauptamt. *Teaching Plan for Worldview Education of the SS and Police*

The soul, which is undeniably of great interest to idealists, became an attractive and mysterious concept, but perhaps, says Nietzsche, the body is even more enticing and mysterious. The body is the most perfect manifestation of the *Will to Power*, the phenomena which we are most clearly now witnessing. Nietzsche's philosophy is basically a song of praise to the reality of the body. It is the philosophy of a true Hellenic instinct.[180]

For National Socialism, the essence of the individual was its biological basis. In the body there was a natural order free from the pollution of abstract theories. Nietzsche called this biological order the "Body's Great Reason". Corporeality itself was *Will to Power*, since human, animal, vegetable, and cellular physiology all act under the pattern of a constant assimilation, taking in surroundings to integrate them into the being. It was an eternal war at every level, from the cellular plane to that of complexly structured organisms. In all this, "Great Reason" took what confronted it, assimilated, and processed it, thus compensating for its own decomposition. For Nazism, without this *Will to Power*, survival was impossible. For the NS Worldview, cells, bacteria, and, in general, every biological entity had no knowledge of philosophical speculations or dogmas of intellectualism, they only acted according to the "Body's Great Reason" and its *Will to Power*, which had always proved successful in preserving life.

New Rational Science

For National Socialism, the modern Western tradition, not content with its already established dualism, further divided mental function in two. On the one hand, the soul, and on the other hand, the spirit or reasoning ability (*Geist*). Like the medieval dualism that placed the soul in a kingdom beyond biological boundaries, Western rationalism did the same with reason.

Western philosophy consistently thought of the mind as a separate entity from the body. Leibnitz established the transmundane home of

---

180 Alfred Bäumler. *Nietzsche, Philosopher and Politician*

the mind in the "monad," a sort of Platonic idea, an entity from which the intellect emanated. Kant placed it on a metaphysical island of "pure reason", a place where the essence of things lived, the so-called "thing in itself". Hegel established that the intellectual consciousness came from an absolute and universal consciousness. The relationship between absolute consciousness and particular consciousness was the so-called "phenomenology of the spirit." For Rene Descartes, the father of Western rationalism, to exist was to think and therefore the essence of man was in the mind. Right as modern science and rationalism were coming to the fore, Nietzsche introduced his concept of the "Body's Great Reason", attributing all human vitality and rationality to biology and the physiological "Great Reason" of the body, his *Will to Power*. National Socialism thus faced-off with the Western scientific tradition and closed ranks with Nietzschean biologism.

For the Nazi philosopher Alfred Bäumler, the Western dualistic separation was only an illusion of the mind that understood itself as being separated from natural reality.

> All reality appears in this distorted and obstructed view: instead of a fighting life, an imaginary world is created in which all is seen through the spiritual values of consciousness. This perspective is also applied to life; existence becomes a monster, something that must be condemned. The error of the philosophers was that they attributed to the unity of consciousness, what really was the unity of force, what Nietzsche called the *Will to Power*.[181]

For Bäumler and his variety of Nietzschean biologism, the ego, the mind or consciousness, was only a part of the whole of man, a part whose importance had been greatly inflated, generating an overloaded individuality, isolated from the world.

In the West, the Self had been understood as the supreme consciousness, the reason-spirit (Geist), the centre of the individual, an unalterable being with the ability to transcend the body. But for Nietzsche, the

---

[181] Alfred Bäumler. *Nietzsche Philosopher and Politician*

modern ego was the opposite of the conscious experience of the *Will to Power*, being rather the introspective repression or redirecting of this will, which instead of being projected into the world, was instead internally repressed. For Nietzsche, the slaves of the Indo-European peoples were the creators of the ego, having been prevented by their masters to from unleashing their *Will to Power* and their creative power, they had fallen into mental processes of internalizing said will. Bäumler also interpreted the internalizing of the *Will to Power* described by Nietzsche as the source of the creation of the Western Self.

> The fundamental error is the absurd overvaluation of the unified consciousness, a being that feels, thinks and wants. This creature is called the mind, the spirit.[182]

For Hitler, the spirit, reason, was a tool of great value that allowed for inventive abstraction as long as it was not lost in musings that distanced it from the *Life-Laws*. For Nazism, this deductive capacity had not been given to man by universal consciousness or by an absolute mind, but had been the result of millennia of evolutionary selection. For Hitler, civilization needed mental processes, logic, and intellectuality, but these processes never had to move away from the physiological laws. National Socialism did not demand irrationality or the loss of instinct, but instead emphasized the necessity of not disconnecting the rational and deductive function of man from the biological reason common to all organisms on earth, that implacable logic based on the laws of existence.

> Generally, strictly material interests will increase to the degree that ideal spiritual viewpoints are disappearing. The more primitive a person is in his spiritual life, the more animalistic he becomes, until in the end he sees obtaining nourishment as the only purpose of life. Thus, a people can indeed endure a certain decrease in material goods as long as supporting ideals are provided as a substitute. But to ensure that these ideals do

---

[182] Alfred Bäumler. *Nietzsche Philosopher and Politician*

National Socialism - Its Principles and Philosophy

not lead to the ruin of a people, they must never take place one-sidedly, at the expense of material nourishment, when the health of the community appears threatened by it. Because a famished people will either physically collapse under the effects of malnutrition or will have to bring about a change in its situation. But physical collapse leads sooner or later to spiritual collapse, and then all ideals vanish as well. Therefore, ideals are healthy and appropriate as long as they help to reinforce a people's inner and collective strength, so that these forces can contribute in carrying out the struggle for survival.[183]

The National Socialist Worldview therefore did not deny reason, but dualistic understanding of it. Ernst Krieck, one of the most important philosophers of the Movement, SS officer, and one of the creators of this new scientific approach, insisted on not falling into the contradiction of creating an irrational science. For the Nazis, science was an abstract product of the evolutionary tool called reason, and as long as it remained in the natural order of the *Life-Laws*, its action would continue to create the important advances and inventions that have allowed human development. Only when the mind fell into the dualistic ideologies and speculative doctrines that abstracted it from its biological reality would this mental tool became a dangerous counter-selective weapon.

> Queen Reason is integrated into a greater totality, of which she is a servant though still an important part of the whole. This is in accordance with the objectives of the future science of National Socialism, whose nature is and will remain within the margins of rational science. Irrational science is a contradiction. But science does not flow from an epistemological truth independent of time and people. Instead, it acts according to a Worldview. Science is not absorbed into the events of the world, situated on an eternal and unchanging island of pure reason, rather, as a result of its objectives, methods, and values, is integrally incorporated into the events of people's lives. Science is not

---
[183] Hitler. Second Book

Heredity Law

based on a mechanical apparatus of purely automated reason, as in the forms of Kantian sensibility, rather its rational foundation and categorical concepts are always limited by the inexhaustible reserve of human existence and race, always reformulating according to the situation and the objectives at hand. There is therefore no pure reason, no absolute science, but rather a form of rationality, science, and epistemological truths valid for a people, a race, a historical situation.[184]

SS Lieutenant Colonel (*SS-Obersturmbannführer*) Dr. Rudolf Frercks, in a text approved with the seal of doctrinal purity, was of the same view as Krieck. For Frercks, intellectual capacity was developed through hereditary foundations along with cultural influences. Meanwhile, for Frercks, Western rationalism always sought to transcend biological reality by placing its origin outside of physiology. And even when Western rationalism took the forms of materialism or monism, it sought an extra-biological plane to explain reason, otherwise rational capacity was subject to genetic determinism, something that Western rationalism rejected categorically.

> The old values of a liberal and unbiological way of thinking collapsed into rubble, and now, as we ask about inborn character, about the biological value of man, we stand at the crossroads between yesterday and tomorrow... Although calculation (Verstand) and the laws of logic may be the same in the whole world, these are only one part of life. That is because during a logical sequence of thoughts not only what I think but what I feel and experience, and above all what I do with it, is very likely different in a German than in, for example, a Jew, and indeed so different that we can conclude based on our experiences that there is a very wide range of differences in the hereditary proclivities and racial composition of these two peoples. Liberal thought called this conclusion unscientific because racial differences, especially in the mental and psychic areas of life, cannot be measured, weighed, or counted, and consequently rejected

---

[184] Ernst Krieck. *The Racial-Völkisch-Political Conception of History*

the evaluation of racial differences among humans and their significance for the course of history and cultures of peoples. The National-Socialist says: "Race is reality, since whenever I go through the world with an open mind I daily observe it and live it, and feel its effects.[185]

For Arnold Gehelen, the philosopher and sociologist of the NSDAP, the search for the origin of reason on an extra-biological plane gave rise to the view of the history of man as a quest to find the metaphysical source of consciousness. Gehelen referred to Hegelian idealism, which described an ever-accelerating journey from primitive consciousness to absolute knowledge, an idea that did not consider that biological decay could alter this path of transcendent enlightenment, leading to intellectual impoverishment.

> It is a high existential experience to formulate relevant new problems, to see them in a new light, to discard those lacking in content that have become conventional, and to reevaluate the meaning behind others long forgotten. But philosophy will not solve those thought patterns that lie behind the false Hegelian doctrine. We have suggested instead the rapid disintegration of that very culture of thought, which is an exhaustion of categories, one could go so far as to call it an extreme impoverishment of confused language, an incomprehensible degeneration of the very same organ which allows for the higher and more profound thought process which have been verified over the last centuries.[186]

The rejection of idealistic dualism and rationalism on the part of the NS Worldview was based on the idea that such thoughts were rooted in German society, and therefore represented problems necessary to solve. But this did not mean a flight from the continental philosophical tradition, the intellectual inheritance of Descartes, Leibnitz, Kant and Hegel, just to end up in the other western theory of mind, the

---

185 Rudolf Frercks. *The Racial Awakening of the German People*
186 Arnold Gehelen. *The State and Philosophy*

English empiricism of Locke and Hume. Nazi genetic determinism clashed drastically with this last philosophical tradition as well, for which man was born with a blank consciousness on which he was imprinting a reality through direct contact between the senses and things, between subject and object. The Nazi Worldview was not empiricist, idealistic, dualistic, monistic, metaphysical, materialist, atomist or postmodernist. These categories reflect schools of thought that had certain parallels, as well as immense differences, with the NS Worldview, so trying to establish intellectual genealogies only leads to confusion. The Worldview was a new philosophical ideology, a new way of thinking.

SPECIAL PATH

For National Socialism, the Racial Policy agenda had to put an end to dualism and reintegrate spirit and the soul into a basic vital unit, subject to the same laws. The *Law of Inheritance*, as well as the *Law of Selection*, had no chance of being fundamental laws for man if they did not act in his living totality. For National Socialism, either reason was a component of biology or it was part of an extra-biological entity, and the latter possibility presented unsolvable scientific problems. This tendency to overcome the mind-body dualism cannot, however, be labeled monism. Monism, or the idea that there is only one universal essence, leads to a materialism that does not do justice to the the Worldview's crusade. National Socialism rather stood as an alternative to materialism and idealism, dualism and monism, a new cultural path where body and soul, or nature and mind, were not based on irreconcilable essences but a shared nature; although in sharing a substance they kept their own defined and autonomous fields of action.

Walther Gross, Chief of Racial Policy of the NSDAP, distinguished National Socialist science as a new biologist approach, distinct from Cartesian science and the metaphysical tradition. Hutton gives account of this new approach:

> Gross stressed holistic unity and the totality of 'life', and rejected the artificial separation of mind and body, as well as

National Socialism - Its Principles and Philosophy

the marginalization of the body in favour of the mental and spiritual, which had left an unhealthy attitude to physical needs and drives, leading to a belief in their sinfulness or their unnatural repression.

Gross's intellectual attack distinguished three kinds of race theory: materialistic or physicalist race theory; [Ludwig] Clauss's mind-body dualism; and National Socialist race theory which was renewing scientific race theory, through the ancient Aryan idea of the unity of mind and body.[187]

This official rejection of dualism was put into practice through the Ministry of Health led by Gerhard Wagner. For Geoffrey Cocks;

Gerhard Wagner harped on the importance of appreciating the totality of the individual and the relationships between body and mind.[188]

For Jay Hatheway, who studied ideology at the SS leadership centres, the vitalist integration of man was the watchword of Nazism.

It was thought that this holistic approach to the individual and his development would produce a unity of body, soul and spirit not unlike the image of the ancient Greeks. Man was considered as a unity, and not divided in body and soul, nor was the people seperate from the State and the culture.[189]

The task of founding a new scientific approach that transcended dualism required a new scientific method. This is the so-called special path (*Sonderweg*) of Nazi science. This path was an alternative to the dualisms between body and mind, life and idea, nature and science, as well as an alternative to materialistic monism. These attempts to unite the two aspects of existence had begun even before Nazism

---

187 Christopher M. Hutton. *Race and the Third Reich*
188 Geoffrey Cocks. *Psychotherapy in the Third Reich*
189 adapted from Jay Hatheway. *In Perfect Formation*

with the reappraisal of Nietzsche and so-called "philosophy of life" (*Lebensphilosophie*). But some of these attempts had aimed at eradicating the importance of mind, the scientific method, or reason, or at least tried to insert the pre-rational content of vital impulses into the scientific method. SS philosopher of education Ernst Krieck already warned that science could not be irrational, since that would be a contradiction. The solution to the problem was therefore not to sacrifice science and reason for the benefit of the instinct, nor was it to endow the rational sphere with irrational content. Without falling into an antagonistic dualism, the Nazi scientific philosophy created a system that maintained clear boundaries between instinct, and reason or mind, while giving both an organic connotation. The philosophical synthesis of this special path was clearly developed by Hugo Dingler, SS officer and philosopher of science.

For Dingler, scientific theory could not be based on abstractions, on detachment of the mind from the world. Theory and method had to be borne of the real world, of the vital impulses, what Dingler called the "primary immediate life." Only then would science have an ethics according to the human nature. It is possible to build scientific scaffolding only on the foundation of the real. For Dingler, this was the Indo-European and Greek method. And although this seemed obvious, it was not a common thing among the flights of the western thought, but the exception. For Western science, only the mind appears as a certain basis. Dingler invited the initiation of a new method, which emanated from this pre-rational source but which would be structured in a rational form. What Dingler called "Method" was a new scientific system emanating from pre-rationality and its vital pulse, but with clear limits established to form a rational foundation. In Dingler's method, mind and nature were united.

For Dingler, science emanated from life in such a way one must always be mindful of the links that allow for the structuring of ideas. Scientific propositions should be based on this vitalist and natural foundation. At the moment a preposition was initiated by the first scientific step, a boundary between life and system would be established. Behind the "System" was the vitalist drive, before it were propositions and scientific scaffolding. These steps were for Dingler iron laws which emanated from the concrete. For him the laws of mechanics, geometry, and classical kinetics discovered with this method, which had been lost with modern science.

The first foundations of method thus consist solely in active operations, in other words, the ability to pre-form them, not in propositions, axioms, precepts, principles, etc... Method is thus not rooted in a metaphysical "mental sphere" but rather in primary immediate life. For, the will to the goal of definite law statements derives from vital life, which precedes all such production of science; the latter is only an instrument, that is, an instrument of life. Similarly, let me also say a word about the extent to which method does and does not take the "I" as its point of departure... method is not rooted in this individual empirical "I"; rather it arises from... the will to attain a growing definite mastery of the real world by means of law statements.

> Thus in the end, method derives from a social goal determination, and arose from within a particular human group, the ancient Greeks and thus the western Indo-Germanic peoples... Since only an "I" can actually carry out the respective individually required actions, the method must formulate its instructions for action from the standpoint of the "I." Nonetheless, method is rooted in those depths from which the ultimate goal determinations of life arise.

From the foundations described we now build stepwise—that is, subsequent steps all resting on previous steps—all those methodical operations for acquiring definite universally valid and objective law statements for the real world that meet our requirements above. We shall call this structure for short 'the system.

A boundary line is indicated here between the fully grounded propositions of the system and all the rest, the "presystematic."... The earlier boundaries were such as between thought and being, mind and matter, idea and reality, etc. While these are often practically very useful and important, they prove on closer inspection to be not entirely sharply defined, indeed not even entirely sharply definable.

Method shows that a third possibility inserts itself between them: the "methodically real." These are the realizations of ideas which we ourselves undertake artificially. They are then not ideas, but they are also not 'nature'... It is nature formed by us according to our ideas.

These laws are *eternal*, that is, they are not subject to change since the elementary building blocks are themselves definite and are unchangeable by the essence of their methodical origin.[190]

For Dingler, the "discovery" of the mind made by the founders of the modern scientific method had given a dualistic foundation to the whole of Western scientific philosophy. The philosophical basis of modern science was based, for Dingler, on the presupposition that the mind was different from natural life, since for modern science the only entity capable of creating science was the rational mind, the Self, the spirit. For Dingler, part of the current methodological error was that these same abstract theories, created out of nothing, were responsible for producing the scientific tools to test themselves. For Dingler, even the most rational scientists of the present, ignoring this philosophical foundation, fell unconsciously into a dualistic, scientific structure where the mind presented itself as a subject detached from nature and its laws. Dingler thought scientific theories had started from the presupposition that the mind had a supernatural capacity to understand reality, a form that transcended the phenomenon and the perceptive chaos of the senses. But for the philosopher of science life itself in its non-dualistic form was in the pre-systemic. In the pre-systemic there was wealth and abundance, the will to life that vitalist philosophies and even Nazi biologism exalted. But Dingler emphatically warned that this vitalist wealth was the strength to set goals and direct the will and not to structure a scientific system. In this field, rationality entered

---

190 Hugo Dingler. *Method instead of Epistemology and Philosophy of Science*

as an evolutionary tool, and yet the communicating vessel was never lost. Nazi science intended to structure itself without losing sight of its biological origin, without searching for its origin on an island of pure reason, but in the depths of the "Body's Great Reason."

> A problem about the relation of thought to being - such as occupied Kant... no longer exists for this [method]. The source of everything immediate, individual, and experienced also lies in the premethodical. Here, I am not yet split up into body and soul... Here I am still a vital unity vis-à-vis all such later conceptual divisions... This primary real bears that characteristic that one today likes to call 'holistic.

> [But] the concept of the holistic cannot be a concept of the system, and that all attempts to make it such must necessarily lead to errors... there is no need to breach with holistic irrationalisms the logical definiteness and consistency of the methodical system.

> Primary life, of which the system is only an instrumental derivative, must be the sole natural place of all holism.

> Whereas Greek antiquity essentially attempted to make assertions about objective being, since Descartes the focus has shifted to the asserter himself and the 'I,' Whereas up to and in the nineteenth century a kind of "pure knowing" was always sought after, in the first third of this century tendencies have become prevalent that place their emphasis on "life." Pragmatism and Lebensphilosophie were the forms of this new wave of thought...

> Although method cannot accept the complete irrationalism and the multiple magic of some tendencies of Lebensphilosophie, it knows quite well that the entire contrivance of science arises out of primary life... that it does not lie in "truths" floating somewhere, which science is supposed to pick out (in inexplicable ways), but that these truths of exact science issue

in the end from the goal-directed willing and acting of the "I," and that they are not, nor need be, a bit less definite, compelling, and exact for this than the ever so rationalistically conceived knowledge of a pure reason and an idealistic realism. The opposition between a one-sided metaphysical rationalism and an equally one-sided chaotic and irrationalistic mysticism of nature has disappeared, since each has delivered its tenable elements, each in its place, to the really tenable system of thought.[191]

---

191 Hugo Dingler. *Method instead of Epistemology and Philosophy of Science*

Twilight of the Idols

For Nietzsche, the revaluation of all values would take place only when dualism, the foundation of the West, was overcome. This Western dualism is understood as being that which was inaugurated by the metaphysics of Socrates and Plato, and later Cartesianism, that is to say, the whole Western mystical tradition, as well as in its subsequent scientific tradition. For Nietzsche, the overcoming of the Western dualism would bring a "Dawn", the start of a new beginning. It would be the triumph of the "human, all too human" over false "Idols". With the "Twilight of the Idols" would come the "Noon of revelation", and man would overcome idealisms and other abstractions of the mind and return to being "faithful to the earth." Certainly these ideas resonated with National Socialism. The overcoming of dualism, the mystical and occult tradition, as well as scientific dualism, were oft-stated goals of many leading Nazi thinkers.

For Alfred Rosenberg, the final triumph of the NS Worldview would occur when biological thought and the laws of existence became the flesh and blood of culture. At a time when each man would think and reason according to these vital laws.

> A political victory alone would never have brought the longed-for real goal of our Movement. If today we wanted to content ourselves only with pure State power, then the National Socialist Movement would not fulfill its mission. We could not have asked so much during these fourteen years of struggle, these great sacrifices, we would not have lasted if men had not given this Movement and their *Führer* their lifeblood, if they had only attempted a mere transfer of political power. Although the political-state revolution is over, spiritual-soul re-foundation, however, is only in its infancy. This important position touches National Socialism in all areas, we call it 'heroic' and we do not,

by any means, understand this as purely militaristic behaviour, but as inner truth, and the courage to answer questions, even if the answers contradict old customs and seemingly settled forms of reasoning. This heroic stance takes off from the creed that blood and character, race and soul are just different designations of the same essence. This was paralleled by the genesis of a new science, a new scientific discovery, which we call raciology. Bodily laws and soul imperatives were investigated and it was found that spirit and body could not be separated from one another, that the laws of bodily inheritance have their direct reflection in psychic disposition and in the inner strength of a particular human group. This new natural knowledge, therefore, is not a simple materialism, like that which we fought all those years. Rather, it signifies a great human awakening after a long hibernation since the end of the ancient Greek world.[192]

The high SS officer Franz Albert Six, argued that understanding the National Socialist Worldview was to think simple, observe nature, and follow its laws. Thus the great cultural barrier to a total assimilation of the NS Worldview lay in the inherent dualism of within the birth of the West.

The revolutionary force of National Socialism is in overcoming the old dualism between matter and spirit, between body and soul. Our enemies brand us as materialists and that our racial thinkers are carried away by a blood mania and by a biological worldview. They assert that the two worlds are opposed here, the racist world and its values of blood and on the other hand the spiritual metaphysics with its moral values. But National Socialism will fight against those who claim that the soul and spirit are hopelessly contrasted with the racial idea or that our Worldview is heretic. All this is pure theory and the National Socialist revolution does not speak of theories but of practical facts. This means changing the worldview of a people from the ominous dualistic contrast to a new holistic view of man.[193]

---

192 Alfred Rosenberg. *Struggle for Our Worldview*
193 Franz Albert Six (under pseudonym Dieter Schwarz). *Attack on the National Socialist Worldview*

Gunther d'Alquen, the popular editor of the SS newspaper "Das Schawrze Korps", was of the same view. Writing in his editorials and articles, approved by the "Personal Staff Reichsführer-SS Main Office":

> The trinity of body, soul, and spirit form a harmonious and living unity in healthy men. But some consider separately these three functions that for us are equivalent. For example, the medieval point of view does not seek legitimacy more than a supposed soul trying to derive the intellectual function of man to the beyond and not giving interest to the body. We also know the tendencies that take no more than the rational spirit and reduce everything to pure mechanics, causality without a soul. These partially false positions are unhealthy because they clash head-on with pure reality. It is a vision that is not as strong as reality and does not coincide with it. It is misfit and unfeasible. The trinity body, soul and spirit form a harmonious unity, and for us equivalent"[194].

Julius Schmidt, SS sub-lieutenant (*SS-Untersturmführer*), reported on the application of this new cultural perspective in the formation of the political elite of the Nazi Reich, a naturalistic approach to existence. "What do chemical formulas have to do with the Worldview? Once the objectives of science were materialistic and mechanistic, others on the contrary were influenced by divine omnipresence. We want the warrior men to feel invested by a mission as scientists.[195].

Hans Günther, one of the most popular racial scholars of the Nazi Reich, was clear in pointing out that the overcoming of Western dualism, both metaphysical, i.e. body and soul separation, and the rationalist dualism that divides man into body and mind, were the great barriers that preclude a real approximation to the laws of existence. And so it was that Western culture sought by rationalistic and metaphysical means to move away from man's animal nature, which brought about a break with natural laws.

---

194 Gunther d'Alquen. *Power and Heart. Das Schwarze Korps*, SS-Hauptamt
195 Julius Schmidt. *Military Science*, SS Troop House. SS-Hauptamt

The further back we go in the history of Indo-Germanic peoples the more we find a traditional focus on inheritance and selection. Our conviction of this inheritance may have been weakened by the penetration of Christian ideas, with their accentuation of the separation of body and soul, spirit and flesh. Where Indo-Germanity perceived more or less consciously and sharply a body-soul unity, Eastern religious forms have taught to separate the body from the soul, the flesh from the spirit. The organic was devalued by Eastern-Christian thinking, presenting it as something of little importance compared to the spiritual. In this way, for the general consciousness, genetic inheritance itself became something that belonged only to lower areas of life and that the spirit could avoid.

It should be emphasized from the outset that a doctrine of hereditary health as a science, whose purpose is the people, simply aims at the elevation of the human being, or more accurately the human being as representing a spiritual-organic unity. We should have no qualms in expressing this fact: the same vital laws apply to the human being as to the animal, unpleasant though it may be for many educated people these days. It is a further effect of the medieval-ecclesiastical separation of body and soul, of flesh and spirit, that today, not a few educated persons before the doctrine of hereditary health speaks contemptuously of breeding of animals or breeding of dogs. It has never seemed plausible to me that the animal is so low that a comparison with man cannot be allowed. The doctrine of hereditary health should give importance provoking the recognition of the dignity of all living things in our people, for only through a grasp of the great laws to which all living things are subjected will it be possible to create a Culture that allows the people to express itself, and seek the means of obtaining the hereditary elevation of the human being.[196]

---

196 Hans F.K. Günther. *People, State, Heritage and Selection*

Spiritual Chaos

For the pre-Socratic philosophers, the source of human vitality resided in the body. This anthropological concept is called hylozoism. The birth of Western European culture put an end to that tradition. Socrates initiated a new stage of Indo-European Being by introducing dualism. His disciple Plato perfected the idea. Plato was initiated into the mystery of the divinity of the soul in Egypt. In Greece he founded an astral religion and granted the human soul a stellar origin.

For Rosenberg, the adoption of metaphysics meant the abandonment of "Germanic religion." Metaphysics was the blow to the psychic plane desired by Socrates in order to dogmatize volitional dynamism in a perennial pair of opposites. For Rosenberg, in the end the Germanic element was too weak to contain the "tide of Syriac-African magic and sorcery," irremediably producing a syncretism of "spiritual chaos, magical cults and the evasion of the world", which resulted in a psychological attitude tending to "see nature as something unreal, like a bad dream"[197].

The history of the adoption of metaphysics was described by Harry Griessdorf, a Nazi intellectual and a writer of ideological textbooks, in his book "Our Worldview" (*Unsere Weltanschauung*), which was given the seal of ideological purity and included in the catalog for the defense of National Socialism.

> With the mysteries came witches and priests who called themselves mystics and initiates, imposing a distinction between priests and laity. The oldest and best known are the Mysteries of Eleusis, also the mysteries of the Cabeiri, a word of Semitic origin. The Great Ecstasy led to the mysteries of Dionysus. This belief is spread from the Near East to Babylon and Egypt. In the Mysteries, strong contrasts are gradually made between God and man, between spirit and flesh, eternity and time, grace and sin, which ultimately leads to asceticism against the body, ecstasy, cleansing of sin, arcane discipline, mystical union, exorcism.

---

[197] Alfred Rosenberg. *The Myth of the Twentieth Century*

National Socialism - Its Principles and Philosophy

For centuries, the Greeks abhorred this kind of orgiastic worship of the gods in the Mysteries, but resistance to the penetration of foreign blood grew weaker, and with that, religious-creative consciousness steadily sank.[198]

For National Socialism, Eastern mysticism contained the whole esoteric ideology of modern spiritual chaos, the so-called "elevation philosophies," schools which were intended to reproduce the mystical experiences of the prophet Ezekiel and his description of the ascension in the divine chariot. Ezequiel-mysticism developed almost a millennium BC, reaching its full flower in first century of the Christian era. It was in this school that a philosophical religious system was first codified based on the metaphysical ascent through subtle planes until union with the divinity. Divine vision, omnipresence, self-deification, universal consciousness, mystical ascension, invocation of angels and other entities, the seven heavens or planes, are all subjects covered by the Merkaba doctrine, a school of Jewish spirituality that later entered Europe in the form of Cabalism during the Renaissance. For National Socialism, this mysticism gave rise to European secret societies, and then during the Enlightenment these sects came to world leadership through republican states charged with masonic esotericism. Later, it would spread through in all spiritist, theosophical, anthroposophical movements and even ariosophy and neo-paganism.

The spiritual attitudes of the Syrian-African mysteries mingled with the Old Testament. The mysteries assumed the feeling of sin, an inner crookedness for which divine mercy was gained through mysticism, secret words and rituals. Dualism made it so that everything bad was attributed to the devil. These concepts, sometimes described with grandiloquence, were reflected in the Jewish apocrypha, the New Testament, and the Gnostics. This continued with the Christian Kabbalists, who acquired prestige in the Renaissance. They read Hebrew texts in an eccentric search for secrets and bizzare visions. Secret societies were formed to blend these fantasies with elements of theology mixed

---

[198] Harry Griessdorf. *Our Worldview*

Twilight of the Idols

with alchemy, mathematics, astronomy, astrology and magic.[199]

For the Nazi intellectuals, all this spiritual chaos led to Christianity, a dualistic syncretism of Indo-European, African, and Asian values. Esoteric Christianity and mysticism structured all of medieval society, giving rise to the archetype of the saint —a social role that did not exist in pre-Christian culture. Furthermore, Polemos that was transformed into the so-called "Holy War," a concept soaked with medieval metaphysics.

> At this time we see a process of general fusion of the ancient world's religions,—a syncretism, the penetration of Eastern gods and worship in the Nordic world. The Mysteries are a destructive force of Afroasiatic origin. The religious attitude of the peoples of Asia and the Phoenician-Etruscans is a desire for the objectification and symbolic representation of the divine. The Myth has been transformed into Mystery. The result is initiate class, the spiritual man, the pneumatic, that is to say, the bearer and agent of the spirit. At the moment the religions of antiquity die, Christianity appears. The union of Christianity with the Mysteries creates Gnosticism. The Gnostics teach a higher Christianity. Christ means the entrance of light into the world. He frees planetary powers from the bindings of evil. Christianity has two principles, therefore, it is dualistic. The Church teaches that creation is born only of the creative will of God, but recognizes a divorce between creator and creature, an insurmountable limit. The Church accepts asceticism, that is, abstinence caused by the dualism of body and soul, world and God. By the escapism and the contempt of corporeity and the fight against the body of flesh, the revulsion at the logical is created. The Christian Church also takes charge of the arcane, occult discipline. This is how the opposites are formed: body and soul, mind and soul, life and death, sin and grace.[200]

---

[199] Franz Alfred Six (Dieter Schwarz). *Freemasonry*
[200] Harry Griessdorf. *Our Worldview*

An anonymous author of the *Guidance Handbooks* of the "SS Main Office" further examined the consequences of mysticism's rejection of man's earthly inheritance.

> The old conception of Antiquity and Christianity establishes a difference between body and soul. They have a different origin: the body is of terrestrial and material origin, the soul of divine and spiritual essence. Each follows a different destiny: the body dies and decomposes, the soul is immortal and continues to live after death. They also have a very contrasted value: the body is a source of instinct, baseness, inferiority and vileness; the soul is the basis of the great and the beautiful, that is, of absolute value. An insurmountable gulf separates them. The body, impure and profane, is what keeps the soul chained down, away from the celestial heights it is destined to soar to. Our Worldview, with its biological principles contradict those views of a decadent and agonizing terrestrial world. We know that these two aspects, soul and body, have been given to us by the Creator. Both are the manifestation of the divine nature, always creative, eternal and active. We know what our ancestors have passed on to us and we will in turn pass the same unto our children. We know that the nobility and purity of our body are also those of our soul. We know that our body and our soul, after all, are only one.[201]

Eidetic Imagery

During National Socialism, mysticism was practically treated as a pathology. The most important psychologist of the National Socialist Reich, Dr. Erich Jaensch, SS officer and early member of the Party, devoted much of his research to studies on the foundations of the mystical psyche. For Jaensch, tendencies of a mystical character had biological roots, and were derived from heritable traits linked to evolutionary strategies very different from those of the Europid human group. Jaensch's research was based on his experiments with so-called eidetic figures. In these experiments volunteers were made

---

201 L. E. Body and Soul, *Guidance Handbooks*, SS-Hauptamt

to view printed images. After the images were removed, a percentage of the individuals presented a strange phenomenon of persistence and continued to see the figures. This was referred to as an eidetic image. Jaensch and his fellow investigators of the eidetic were very clear in pointing out that this perception was not a posterior image of the figure, nor a mental representation, memory or hallucination. The eidetic image was a real and three-dimensional visualization that was perceived as a concrete object. Individuals who presented the perception of eidetic images more acutely actually saw such objects, and could describe details at any angle in a psychophysical process equivalent perception of a real object.

> Jaensch's research found that eidetic types were less likely to structure perceptual chaos and that their objectification of reality was more subjective, because the contents of consciousness were not so firmly fixed. In these eidetic psychological types the asymmetries of conscious and practical life, where one thing was distinctly different from another, disappeared, their logical faculty failing to maintain the difference and diversity of the world. According to Jaensch's research, the eidetic type or "integrated" type tended to create unreal images, compared to the "non-integrated" type who tended to process the world as it was. For Jaensch, this process had no relation to creative capacity or imagination, but was rather a different way of perceiving reality, an evolutionary path that led to a particular epistemology. For Jaensch, the "integrated" perception of human groups outside the Indo-European cultural sphere was responsible for the tendencies towards mysticism and dualistic metaphysics, a tendency that was widely spread throughout Europe by migrations and historical developments.

> The difference between integrate and disintegrate types also includes the distinction between northern and southern types, which has been drawn by race biologists. That integration (in our sense) is 'sun adaptation' which has been proved by investigations of the color sense of integrates and disintegrates... there is an unequivocal correlation between psycho-physical integration

and redsightedness, which has been proved to be a sign of sun adaptation... Persons with dark eyes, dark skin and dark hair were predominantly 'redsighted.' We cannot as yet generalize... But some correlation between dark pigmentation and integrate structure is certainly evident from our investigations as a whole.

Professor A. Encinas, Santander visited us last year in order to be introduced to eidetics, because he hoped that it would provide some clue to the phenomena that are being talked about a great deal in Spain at the moment. Hundreds of sworn statements have been made to the effect that certain pictures of saints perform miracles, step out of their panels, carry out actions, etc. These assertions are based in particular on sworn statements by scientifically educated persons, like engineers, doctors, etc. who are accustomed to sober thinking. We demonstrated the peculiarities of perceptive processes in eidetic subjects to our Spanish colleague. What he saw strengthened his supposition that these peculiarities were the key to the phenomena in Spain.[202]

Spirit or Blood

National Socialism grounded its anti-dualist Worldview on the religious attitudes of the Indo-European past. For Hans F. K. Günther, one of the most prominent Nazi researchers of Indo-European culture, this people experienced their existence in constant evolution and founded their cultural order on nature and its laws.

> The Indo-Europeans believed...in a succession without end or beginning, of world origins and world endings, in repeated twilights of the Gods and in renewals of the world and of the Gods in a grandiose display, exactly as is described in the *Völuspa* of the *Edda*. They believed in repeated cataclysms, such as the Hellenes described, upon which new worlds with new Gods would follow. A succession of world creations and world

---

[202] Erich Jaensch. *Eidetic Imagery*

endings was taught by Anaximandros, Heraclitus, Empedocles and other Hellenic thinkers, and later by the Roman poet and thinker Lucretius.

No religiosity which declares the world and man to be valueless, low and unclean, and which wishes to redeem man to over-earthly or superhuman sacred values, is truly Indo-European. Where "this world" is dropped, and in its place the "other world" is raised to eternal good, there the realm of Indo-European religiosity is abandoned. For Indo-European religiosity is of this world, and this fact determines its essential forms of expression. As a result it is sometimes difficult for us to comprehend its greatness today...We are today accustomed to seek true religiosity only in terms of the other world and to regard religiosity of this world as undeveloped or lacking in some aspect—a preliminary stage on the way to something more valuable.

Whoever wishes to measure religiosity... by the degree to which man feels a cleft between a transitory body and an indestructible soul, between flesh (sarx) and spirit (pneuma)—whosoever seeks to do this will have to declare that the religiosity of the Indo-Europeans is truly impoverished and paltry.

A perceptive form of theoretical dualism, in which the subject faces the object—in which the perceiver faces an "object of perception"—will be no more to the true Indo-European spirit, than a method, a convenient thought process for knowledge, and he will neither emphasize the concept of contrast between body and soul nor will he misjudge (as did Ludwig Klages) the spirit aroused in the tension between the subject and object as an adversary of the soul. To the Indo-European, the distinction between body and soul is not stimulating, not even to religiosity.

Quite remote from them lies the idea that the body, addicted to this world, is a dirty prison for a soul striving out of it towards another world...For this reason, every idea of killing the senses, of asceticism, lies very remote from this race, and would appear to them as an attempt to paralyze rather than balance human nature.[203]

Harald Spehr, SS officer and member of the Reich Main Security Office was on the same track in establishing the characteristics of the Eastern mystery and the danger it posed for the culture that National Socialism sought to create.

> "Willful abandon, intoxication, ekstasis, the sacred orgy, out-of-body experiences and willful wallowing in the psychic spheres of other men are characteristic traits of the Near Eastern racial soul; moderation, metron, temperamantia are characteristic traits of the Nordic racial soul and of aboriginal Indo-Germanic piety, eusebeia as a cognate of sophrosyne." Here we have an attempt to discard the Germanic worldview built on the standards of heroic honor and propriety in favor of a magical worldview.[204]

The National Socialist Worldview was oriented precisely as the opposite of the ascending mystery cult. The focus of Nazi spirituality was rooted in the earth. His transcendental pursuit was aimed at meeting the God of life and the laws of nature.

> The guiding idea of the medieval Christian orders was the elevation of the soul, the liberation of the body for the union of the soul with a god in the Beyond. The Order of Clans of the SS, is founded in the heart of the National Socialist Movement on a totally new basis. The essential criterion of our Order is the obligation to marry! We consider wife selection, permanent selection as the means to improve life. We do not need to be ascetics, for we do not want a god from beyond! Our creed, the "incarnation" and consequently the proper destiny of the God of life, is achieved by way of the evolution of species, for we do not want a God from beyond, our God asks us to be earthly,

---

203 Hans F. K. Günther. *The Religious Attitudes of Indo-Europeans*
204 Harold Spehr. *Were the Ancient Germans "Ecstatics"?*

for the world as we know it is his field of action, his body. Thus the SS, as a God-believing order (*gottgläubiger Order*), of the National Socialist Worldview of the twentieth century, is an earthly order in the highest sense of the word. The time of error has passed.[205]

National Socialism sought to reverse the mysterious influence of the last millennia, to end dualism and free the human psyche from confrontation with nature and mental solipsism. In his book *The Voice of the SS: A History of the SS Journal Das Schwarze Korps*, William Combs devotes a whole chapter to the so-called "Dispute between spirit and blood" (*Geist oders Blut*), the crusade of National Socialism against superstition and occultism. The position defended by the SS was to replace metaphysical mysticism with a religiosity of the earth and its sacred laws of struggle and eternal renewal. The SS could not be called atheistic, however much of its approach to the sacred was steeped in a realistic look at the *Life-Laws*. The religious approach of the SS was biologist, grounding its transcendental character in the people as supra-historical and eternal, a Worldview that provided a balm to the irremediable end of life in projecting the individual into descent and community preservation.

> Certainly our religion, our faith in our people and their future has been anchored in the real. We believe in eternity in the same way as religious Christians. We believe that the forces that have allowed our people to escape death are as religious as those representations that almost shrouded under medieval dogmas form the true nucleus of the current religious doctrine.[206]

National Socialism is sometimes associated with the occult. Perhaps much of this comes from the dramatic ceremonies of National Socialism, its exotic symbols, and the rumors of the hidden practices of some of its leaders.

---

205 J. Mayerhofer. *The Order of the Clans. Guidance Notebooks,* SS-Hauptamt
206 Gunther d'Alquen. *The Spiritual Crisis. Guidance Notebooks, SS-Hauptamt.*

Hitler's public speeches however leave little doubt about his attitude to the occult. On September 6, 1938, in a speech in Nuremberg, he said:

"We will not allow people with mystical beliefs, to explore the secrets of the world beyond. These people are not National Socialists."

A few articles with a supernatural theme in the SS newspaper does not confirm a Nazi belief in occultism. Its approach is rational and scientific. *Das Schwarze Korps* went even further and carried out a prominent campaign against all sorts of superstition and occultism. This is a surprising policy taking into account that officially the newspaper was the voice of Himler, the Reichsführer of the SS. This raises doubts about whether the rumors about him are real or whether his interest in the occult has been greatly exaggerated. *Das Schwarze Korps'* sustained and determined campaign against mysticism and the occult would be a rather strange policy for a journal that professes absolute loyalty to Hitler and Himmler if these leaders were in fact sympathetic to the occult. There is no doubt that the editors of the SS newspaper permanently sought Himmler's guidance on how to deal with these issues, and yet there is no indication that Himmler would oppose or restrict the newspaper's campaign against the occult.[207].

CRUSADE AGAINST MYSTICISM

In the Nazi ideology the mysteries of nature, poetic inspiration, and the mythical were products of the blessings of the natural order, and never understood as magical acts that revealed powers from beyond. The revaluation of the traditions of the Germanic and Indo-European past by the heritage research institutes of the SS are to be understood from this perspective. Hitler was clear about this, and through speeches and executive orders led the crusade against mystical deviationism within National Socialism:

---
207 Williams Combs. *The Voice of the SS*

Twilight of the Idols

National Socialism is not a sect or movement of worship, but exclusively a popular political doctrine based on racial principles. In its purposes there is no mystery cult, only the concern to lead the people. Therefore, we have no temples for worship, only walls for the people. We do not have open spaces of worship, but spaces for assemblies and parades. We do not have religious retreats, but arenas for field games and the main feature of our meeting places is not the mystical brilliance of the cathedral but the brightness of a room that combines beauty and fitness for its purpose. In these spaces, there are no acts of worship, but they are exclusively dedicated to the gathering of people who have come to know each other in the course of our struggle. We will not let occultists and mystics with passion to explore the secrets of beyond, to take possession of our Movement. These people are not National Socialists, but something else, in any case something that has nothing to do with us. At the head of our program there are no secret meetings, but a clear vision.

There was a time when semi-obscurity was needed for the effectiveness of certain teachings. Today, we live in an age where light is a fundamental condition for success. It would be a sad day if these mystical and obscurantist elements co-opted the Movement or the State, leading hidden councils. It would even be dangerous to imagine some kind of place of worship, because in its construction it would be necessary to think of religious rites that have nothing to do with National Socialism. Our worship is exclusively to cultivate the natural— and since it is natural, it is divine will. Our humility is unconditional submission to the divine laws of existence as they are known to man, to them we respectfully entrust ourselves. Our commandment is the resolution to perform our tasks according to these laws."[208]

Hitler referred in his speech to the innumerable mystic currents of Neopaganism that struggled to influence the politics of the Nazi Reich. They had come to collaborate through nationalist groups

---

208 Hitler. *Cultural Speech in Nuremberg, September 6, 1938*

absorbed by the initial political syncretism of the Movement. Some of these deviationists achieved some popularity among the base of Nazism. Gunther d'Alquen, the editor of the official SS newspaper, constantly denounced the damage caused by mixing the NS Worldview with these ideas. "In this case, the national reality, the racial idea and, in short, our love for this world becomes an illusion without foundation that gives way to considerations that analyze the people in a metaphysical or scholastic way; Chimeric speculations and a falsification of the mystical sense of national reality. This nationalistic mysticism acts through sainted and intolerant representatives. Its conceptions are based on the customs, traditions, runic gymnastics and mysterious magic. They meet in sects, they loathe clear concepts. Science and economics represent for them only liberal concepts, and inventions of the devil.[209]

One of these racial mystics was Ludwig Clauss, theorist of the Nordic soul and author of popular books of metaphysical speculations. Clauss was a member of the Party and at one point dreamed of hegemonizing Racial Policy with his theories. For Clauss, the body and the soul were entities of different essence. In his doctrine, the existence of a spiritual race parallel to the biological physical race was defended. With time, Clauss rejected any importance of biological laws in the human essence. Walter Darré, SS General and former combatant of the NSDAP, in his 1930 work "Race, a new nobility of blood and soil", was already warning about the dangers Claussian dualism posed to the racial theory of National Socialism.

> Errors about the link between spirit and matter occur in the racial domain. This error probably has its origin in the works of Clauss. The ideas of Clauss have acted upon a circle of men for whom the affirmation of a distinction between race and soul would allow to evade the material laws of their own race. Unfortunately, the works of Clauss have caused an impression that he did not foresee. This is worrying. Some of the readers

---

[209] Gunther d'Alquen. *Power and Heart.* "*Das Schwarze Korps*", SS-Hauptamt

believe that it is possible to evade the experimentally established scientific facts of the doctrine of race and heredity, seeing in it nothing more than materialism. Speaking of materialism, they see themselves as idealists. Whether seeking the legitimacy of heredity in matter, in the body, or in an unknown force like the soul, we must necessarily preserve the material laws of heredity. The dispositions of the soul are therefore equally hereditary.[210]

The Movement's attempts to establish it's scientific basis clashed strongly with Clauss's theory. Walter Gross, in charge of racial matters in the NSDAP, attacked him especially harshly. In 1938, confident in his popularity, Clauss asked the internal court of the NSDAP to make a judgment on the attacks from Gross. The court's determination however, was categorical. Clauss was accused of attacking the NS Worldview and was declared unfit to direct any aspect of Racial Policy because of his subjective theories. He was subsequently expelled from the Party and from official positions in government.

AKTION HESS

But the crusade against dualism and mysticism took its hardest turn in the so-called *Aktion Hess,* the popular name for the "Campaign against occult doctrines and so-called occult sciences." This police operation under SS command was ordered to remove all types of organizations and groups of a mystical nature. The operation was framed within the investigation that sought to clarify the inexplicable trip of Rudolf Hess to England in the middle of the war. This investigation revealed that the *Führer's* lieutenant had been persuaded to make his journey with occult arguments. The *Aktion Hess* closed all kinds of lodges, orders and esoteric organizations. Almost a hundred initiatory groups and a thousand New Age prophets, astrologers, mystics, and messiahs were imprisoned. Peter Staudenmaier, a scholar of Anthroposophy (one of the doctrines under attack) describes this operation:

---

210 Walter Darré. *Race, a new nobility based on Blood and Soil*

National Socialism - Its Principles and Philosophy

On June 9, 1941, less than two weeks before Germany invaded the Soviet Union, the Nazi domestic security services launched an all-out campaign against occultist organizations, practices, and individuals. Officially dubbed the "Campaign against occult doctrines and so-called occult sciences" (*Aktion gegen Geheimlehren und sogenannte Geheimwissenschaften*), this intensive effort aimed at the definitive elimination of occult activities and beliefs from the Volksgemeinschaft, the German national community.

> There had long been a hard-line anti-occultist faction within the Nazi movement, concentrated above all in the SD, the Sicherheitsdienst or 'security service' of the SS... Heydrich's SD had hounded a wide variety of occultist tendencies since the early days of the Third Reich... The SD's enduring hostility toward occult groups and esoteric doctrines stemmed in part from the perceived organizational competition that such currents represented, but the anti- occultist faction of the SD viewed occult tendencies above all as an ideological threat to the integrity of National Socialist principles. In the eyes of the SD, occultists belonged, willingly or not, to the broad panoply of weltanschauliche Gegner or ideological enemies of Nazism.
>
> By June 1941, the ire of the SD, the Gestapo, and their allies such as Bormann and Propaganda Minister Joseph Goebbels was not just directed at anthroposophists but theosophists, ariosophists, astrologists, parapsychologists, fortune tellers, faith healers, rune readers, dowsers, and a myriad of other believers in, or practitioners of, supposed occult arts.[211]

Aktion Hess marked the triumph of the anti-dualist faction of National Socialism. From the time of this operation there were no longer any doubts as to the ideological course of Nazism. Hitler imposed his vision and the SS purified its ideology, closing ranks with the *Führer*.

For Hitler, the triumph over dualism and mysticism was opening up

---

211 Peter Staudenmaier. *Between Occultism and Fascism*, 354-355.

Twilight of the Idols

a new spiritual approach to the mysteries of life, this time under the valuation of the Life Laws and not under the metaphysical doctrines of the West. Hitler hoped that this process would be gradual, framed as a cultural exchange, not forced but taken up honestly due to the triumph of scientific culture. For Hitler, only by abandoning superstitions and religious doctrines could the *Life-Laws* be assumed as cultural truths, without the need to abandon spiritual concerns and belief in God. This would be the path of National Socialism towards the definitive implementation of the *Life-Laws*:

> I'm convinced that any pact with the Church can offer only a provisional benefit, for sooner or later the scientific spirit will disclose the harmful character of such a compromise. Thus the State will have based its existence on a foundation that one day will collapse.
>
> An educated man retains the sense of the mysteries of nature and bows before the unknowable. An uneducated man, on the other hand, runs the risk of going over to atheism (which is a return to the state of the animal) as soon as he perceives that the State, in sheer opportunism, is making use of false ideas in the matter of religion, whilst in other fields it bases everything on pure science.
>
> That's why I've always kept the Party aloof from religious questions...If anyone has needs of a metaphysical nature, I can't satisfy them with the Party's program. Time will go by until the moment when science can answer all the questions... So it's not opportune to hurl ourselves now into a struggle with the Churches. The best thing is to let Christianity die a natural death... All that's left is to prove that in nature there is no frontier between the organic and the inorganic.
>
> Originally, religion was merely a prop for human communities. It was a means, not an end in itself... The instructions of a hygienic nature that most religions gave, contributed to the foundation of organized communities. The precepts ordering

people to wash, to avoid certain drinks, to fast at appointed dates, to take exercise, to rise with the sun, to climb to the top of the minaret—all these were obligations invented by intelligent people. The exhortation to fight courageously is also self-explanatory...

It's possible to satisfy the needs of the inner life by an intimate communion with nature, or by knowledge of the past. Only a minority, however, at the present stage of the mind's development, can feel the respect inspired by the unknown, and thus satisfy the metaphysical needs of the soul. The average human being has the same needs, but can satisfy them only by elementary means.

We, for our part, confine ourselves to asking man to fashion his life worthily. For this, it is sufficient for him to conform to the laws of nature. Let's seek inspiration in these principles, and in the long run we'll triumph over religion.

It's possible to satisfy the needs of the inner life by an intimate communion with nature, or by knowledge of the past. Only a minority, however, at the present stage of the mind's development, can feel the respect inspired by the unknown, and thus satisfy the metaphysical needs of the soul. The average human being has the same needs, but can satisfy them only by elementary means...The person whose life tends to simplification is thirsty for belief, and he dimly clings to it with all his strength.

Nobody has the right to deprive simple people of their childish certainties until they've acquired others that are more reasonable. Indeed, it's most important that the higher belief should be well established in them before the lower belief has been removed. We must finally achieve this. But it would serve no purpose to replace an old belief by a new one that would merely fill the place left vacant by its predecessor.

It seems to me that nothing would be more foolish than to reestablish the worship of Wotan. Our old mythology had ceased to be viable when Christianity implanted itself. Nothing dies unless it is moribund. At that period the ancient world was divided between the systems of philosophy and the worship of idols. It's not desirable that the whole of humanity should be stultified.

A movement like ours mustn't let itself be drawn into metaphysical digressions. It must stick to the spirit of exact science. It's not the Party's function to be a counterfeit for religion.

If, in the course of a thousand or two thousand years, science arrives at the necessity of renewing its points of view, that will not mean that science is a liar. Science cannot lie, for it's always striving, according to the momentary state of knowledge, to deduce what is true. When it makes a mistake, it does so in good faith. It's Christianity that's the liar. It's in perpetual conflict with itself.

One may ask whether the disappearance of Christianity would entail the disappearance of belief in God. That's not to be desired. The notion of divinity gives most men the opportunity to concretize the feeling they have of supernatural realities. Why should we destroy this wonderful power they have of incarnating the feeling for the divine that is within them? The man who lives in communion with nature necessarily finds himself in opposition to the Churches. And that's why they're heading for ruin.

I especially wouldn't want our movement to acquire a religious character and institute a form of worship. It would be appalling for me, and I would wish I'd never lived, if I were to end up in the skin of a Buddha![212]

---

212 Hitler. *Table Talk*

Twilight of Men

Almost twenty years after writing *Mein Kampf*, Hitler gave a speech to a group of officer cadets. The foundations of the Worldview remained unchanged. Perpetual struggle, selection, heredity and fertility were again the foundations of the NS Worldview that the *Führer* attempted to pass on to his warriors. Helmut Helber, who compiled this speech, attributes these themes to a desperate call on the part of Hitler for his officers to sacrifice themselves in a war that was already lost.

> The speech given by Hitler to the officers of different divisions share in general the same thought. In the eleven speeches which have come to us, we see Hitler explaining for the umpteenth time his theory of the struggle for life.[213]

But what we really find in these speeches is a synthesis of the laws of the Worldview. Hitler held out to his warriors the possibility of becoming part of the universal order. It was in the Great War that the *Führer* saw the reality of the world, without ideals or ideological constructions, and Hitler prepared his warriors to experience that same revelation.

> We are all creatures of nature, who if you take a comprehensive look only know one law, the right to live for he who triumphs in the struggle. Humans cannot escape this law. Following this eternal law, planets revolve around suns and moons around planets. In both the greatest and the smallest this basic principle dominates: that the strongest determines the way. In our land, we see the constant struggle of beings with each other. We can say our world is cruel; the existence of some involves the destruction of others. Spiritually we can get away from this world, but the

---

213 Helmut Heiber. *The Führer Speaks*

truth is that we are entirely a part of it. Any withdrawal means death. One can repeat a thousand times: "my intention is good," but nature, Providence, does not ask opinions or intentions, and only knows one law: Fight, man! Do what you must to survive. Do not fight, and you will die. He who does not accept this law denies the laws of the existence of all beings. We do not shy away from this law, however painful it may be. Nature grants living beings the impulse to multiplication, conservation and propagation of the species and nature does not obstruct these, rather their limitation arises because of the struggle for existence, out of the force of the beings themselves.

Whoever renounces these laws, renounces Providence. And since this fundamental principle has not been established by man, rather, human beings are only small things forced to live with it, this principle is the will of Providence. And no person has ever existed who could have imagined a better structuring of the existence of beings. There is no other substitute imaginable than the principle of the eternal selection of the best. And when someone says, "but this small and magnificent people has sunk despite wanting peace," it is because nature does not ask for intention, but only for power.

A people who lack the power to prevail in life also lack, according to the eternal laws of nature, justification to continue living. This is reflected daily on this earth in hundreds of thousands, and millions of individual struggles between beings. And it will continue to be so. If the people observe the natural laws of the propagation of the species, it can be said that communities must necessarily grow in number. And if, by increasing its population, the extent of its living space is not changed, over time there will always be a disproportion between the growing population and the unaltered living space. This can only be avoided by taking certain measures. Either the members of the community begin to emigrate, or they take a more radical decision: the reduction of the birth rate. However, this way of adapting a growing population to the unaltered living space is particularly frightening, since then all the selection process is finished. This reduction is totally opposite to the process of natural selection.

When man limits the birthrate he carries out a completely stupid action, because he kills something without knowing the implications. If our ancestors had observed this practice, the artificial limitation of births, then, compatriots, we would not be here, we would have actually ceased to be a people, for the importance of a people lies in its great men, which, through their leadership, shape the existence of nations. Culture is also exclusively based on those wonderful minds, gifts for their people, who as creators and configurators of a more beautiful human existence are of inestimable value for the world in which they live. Let us ask the question: Are these people always the first born or the second born? Perhaps, to our astonishment, we must respond in this way: Never! In a large number of cases it is not even the third or fourth, but the sixth, seventh, eighth, tenth, eleventh, and sometimes even the thirteenth or the fourteenth child. All our great thinkers, our poets, our musicians, our statesmen and our military leaders, and so on, have almost never been the first or the second child. So they would never have been born! And it can not be said: "Then others would come forward." No, they cannot come at all, because man would be excluding the indispensable condition for the selection process.[214]

This speech reflects the concern of the Reich authorities for securing the Worldview as much as possible. In 1944, despite enormous restrictions on the availability of paper for book production, all the agencies of the Movement made a last effort to instill in the population, German and European, the spirit of the National Socialist Worldview. The SS published the important textbook *"Teaching Plan for Worldview Education of the SS and Police"* (*Lehrplan für die Weltanschauliche erziehung in der SS und Polizei*). The Army did the same, publishing *"Why Do We Fight"* (*Wofür Kämpfen Wir?*) in an indoctrination effort carried out under the supervision of both Hitler and Rosenberg. The

---

214 Hitler. *Cadets Speech 1942*

last stage of the war also saw the appearance of the fundamental text *"Struggle as Life-Law"* (*Kämpf als Lebensgesetz*), attributed to the philosopher Harry Griessdorf and published by "NS-Leaders Team of the Army High Command" (*NS-Führungsstab der Oberkommando Der Wehrmacht*).

The *"Teaching Plan for Worldview Education of the SS and Police"* was an effort to diffuse the Worldview across Europe through the multicultural Waffen-SS, deployed in the many theaters of the war. The *Life-Laws* were to be understood and assumed by the whole continent in a new pan-European political-economic order:

> This curriculum was created taking into account the fact that, today, volunteers from almost all European countries serve in Waffen-SS. The teaching plan is therefore for units of the Germanic Reich, as well as for units with elements from Western and Eastern Europe. The European community has two common inheritances. First, a biological inheritance and second, a common struggle for centuries, a cultural and historical heritage.[215]

The book went into detail about what it called "the foundations of our Worldview, based on the *Life-Laws*." In the text all the laws of the Worldview were reviewed once again. Special emphasis was given to evolutionary thinking, which was described as a fundamental element in the understanding the *Life-Laws*. It is incredible to think that in the most decisive moment of the struggle, in the midst of World War II, National Socialism gave so much importance to the mass-instruction of its soldiers in the foundations of the Worldview, giving a knowledge of biology and evolution to men who in many cases had only basic education, and were absorbed in the difficulty of battle, deprivation and constant retreat and defeat.

> The *Life-Laws* lead to the conclusion that man is a unity of body, soul and spirit, interacting only by the harmony of all these

---

[215] SS-Hauptamt. *Teaching Plan for Worldview Education of the SS and Police*

forces that represent the typical human quality. Non biological systems divide this unity and build its world, either in the purely material, or seek only the soul and spirit and are therefore forced to despise the flesh. The doctrine of evolution, that is, the knowledge of the relation of all living beings, determines that man is fully immersed in natural events. And just as the earth has not always been as we see it today, so life over it has undergone innumerable changes of form. From simple forms the current variety has been developed. Memories of the early stages of development remain the atrophied organs, that is, those that were likely to reach a weak level of development, but are no longer able to fulfill their original function, such as the appendix, wisdom teeth, the fold in the eye and eyelid. The immense wealth of forms in nature is an expression of the evolutionary capacity of organisms. We can demonstrate this by cultivating plants and domestic animals, and by the fact that sudden erratic alterations that prove to be heritable, the so-called mutations, occur. The hereditary condition of the ability to change is a direct proof of the mutability of organisms. Procreation, reproduction and inheritance are the basic facts of the evolution of life on Earth. These are prerequisites for further conservation. For the teaching of the *Life-Laws* it is necessary that these basic precedents be known by all of us, at least in their principal characteristics.[216]

Subsequently, the text dealt with issues of cell biology and genetics, chromosomes, cells, relationship with the environment, the inexhaustible fertility of nature and different fertility rates according to the conditions of the environment, the influence of rural or urban environments, mental and biological diseases in the world and other aspects necessary, for understanding the solid scientific foundation of the *Life-Laws*.

Why Do We Fight? (*Wofür Kämpfen Wir?*), was published in 1944 by special mandate of Hitler as a means of transferring to the officers of

---

216 SS-Hauptamt. *Teaching Plan for Worldview Education of the SS and Police*

National Socialism - Its Principles and Philosophy

the Army the motivations of the struggle. Although at times it adopts a more traditional tone, different to the one used with the SS troop, the Worldview fully gravitates. In *Why Do We Fight?* it was clearly stated that war was the death struggle between Worldviews. The Reich's naturalistic Worldview against the puritanical, imperialist, and plutocratic worldview of England and North America, coupled with the Marxist worldview of the Soviet Union, both as an expression of the Jewish worldview and its messianic objectives. The text had an introduction signed by the Fuehrer who gave the approval of the publication and ordered its massive distribution on the front as a way to motivate a fight to death.

> I have ordered the Army to publish a text that will decide on the vital issues of the German people, not only in the military area, but also in all aspects of the Worldview, to achieve an unconditional agreement between State and official leadership. The book *Why Do We Fight?* must give the officer an orientation of the Worldview and intellectual skills for political education and training of soldiers. I have, therefore, ordered this book to include the thought of the Worldview.[217]

In *Why Do We Fight?*, struggle, selection, inheritance and abundance are once again the laws that allowed for preservation, laws that decided the future of the people more categorically than economic and political theories. The text asked soldiers and officers for the maximum sacrifice in the defense of the NS Worldview in a call whose echo meant the maximized effort in the defense of the Reich. The text was very explicit and was distributed on a large scale. The Reich troops fought and died for an intimately assimilated Worldview.

> Belief in the divine universal order and the progress of man is the expression of our Worldview. This belief is the instinctive force of all our acts. But to have a clear Worldview this should not contradict scientific knowledge and laws. As Germanic men we must be certain that our belief is verifiable, that it

---
217 Army Personnel Office. *Why Do We Fight?*

can be put into practice and that it is fit for life. The book *On the Omnipotence and Order of Life* SS-Sturmbannführer Dr. Stengel von Rutkowski says:

Being the world a creation of the divinity, the *Life-Laws* must be divine as well. That is why racial thought is the most important knowledge. Therefore, the scientific, political and ideological care of natural science and of life is for us in the first place. For us, life, race, work, nature, Nation, have the highest values not because of an arbitrariness, but because all these things lead by the path of divinity, the meaning of life, a vital order ". We regard the struggle as an irrefutable law of life. Only in the struggle do the conditions of selection, the personality grow and a strong people are created. Only in the struggle we are born for greatness. The Germanic man gives shape to his life by fighting. The struggle accompanies him in all his existence. Fight fate, fight against a threatening environment. In countless confrontations he becomes master of his destiny. The struggle is the divine law with which the German is formed and educated for strength. The struggle is the great element of National Socialism, the worldview of combative man. We know from the *Life-Laws* that there are three dangers to the conservation of a town, a low birth rate, counter-selection and mixing. We must follow the victory of the arms the victory of the children. We must follow the biological process of selection and not counter-selection. The correct choice of the couple is the only way to give value to the clan. Although a people is not only characterized by race, but by history, living space, language, the racial foundation is decisive. The National Socialist Worldview gives the people the highest known value, it is the basic substance for the selection.[218]

On the other hand, the book *Struggle as Life-Law* (*Kämpf als Lebensgesetz*), the last chapter of a series of texts edited by the section in charge of the Worldview in the Army, was one of the most direct texts when it comes to treating life as a struggle and how to assimilate this

---

218 Army Personnel Office. *Why Do We Fight?*

principle without entering a culture of barbarism. The text reviewed the human warrior ethic and its differences with the instinct of animal struggle, also established certain foundations to better assimilate this law of life. "Struggle does not forgive weak hearts", " Struggle is the father of all things", " Struggle leads to order and life in community", "Man has been placed in the struggle", "Man Struggle for ideals", "Struggle creates peoples and races" and "If you do not risk life you will never make a living ", are some of the issues addressed in the text, in an effort to ensure that the Reich troops correctly assimilate the warrior ethic in a modern society with a collaborative spirit. The struggle was presented in the text as an irrevocable destiny. At times, it adopted characteristics of a struggle for progress and sometimes a real struggle against enemies. The war was presented as the destructive side of the struggle, a life-and-death test for preservation. Incredible as it may seem, these texts were not war propaganda, but rather were manuals that delivered a Worldview to the soldier, a vision of the world that allowed them to make sense of their participation in combat.

> In the nature, in the history of our people, both in the individual and in the community, the *Law of Struggle* remains true for all creatures. Even if outwardly times of peace alternate with times of struggle. No one can escape the will of Providence. Eternal creation determines struggle as the law of life. The people entered this war with the clear conviction that has been inevitable, which must be fought hard, gathering every piece of strength. With these thoughts we fight today for the future of our people. From the forces of our blood and from the heroic example of our ancestors we accept the struggle; we accept the ancient *Law of Struggle*. We affirm the sacrifices of war and understand that death is a prerequisite for the future of our people. Without struggle there is no freedom, without struggle there is no life, the one who wants to live must fight.[219]

The last expression of the Nazi Worldview is found in Hitler's political

---

219 NS Leadership Staff of the High Command of the Armed Forces. *Struggle as Life Law*

testament. Written hours before his death, the *Führer* blamed the war on the Allied nations and international Jewry, then announced his plan to remain in Berlin and his decision to die with Eva Braun. He glorified the heroic people and fighters of the Reich and then proceeded to restructure the government. In his last sentence, Hitler asked of the leaders of National Socialism *"the scrupulous observation of the laws of race"*.

THE DEFEAT OF THE WORLDVIEW

Nietzsche invites one to be human, leaving aside flights of the mind and fantasy. Thus he demands we remain faithful to the earth. National Socialism echoed this call, without a doubt. Being "human, all too human" had the effect of overcoming metaphysical and dualist man, Western man.

> Let the Superman be the meaning of the earth. I exhort you to remain faithful to the earth, and not to believe those who speak to you of super-earthly hopes. They despise life, the earth is tired of them. In other times the soul despised the body, the soul preferred a thin, ugly, hungry body. In this way he thought to sneak out of the body, and the Earth.[220]

The defeat of the National Socialist Reich meant the "decline of men", the end of the attempt to overcome Western man, the decline of the "human, all too human" and, in Nietzsche's words, the triumph of the "idols."

The embryo of the new Nazi man was aborted, defeat in the war dashed all hopes of overcoming Western culture under the aegis of this Worldview. None of the original ideologues continued their work after the defeat. But no single one of them was fundamental. The creator of the NS Worldview was Hitler, but its elaboration was collective, taking place within the institutional framework of the Movement. The political and cultural conditions that had somehow incubated and gave

---

[220] Nietzsche. *Thus Spoke Zarathustra*

birth to the Nazi Worldview completely vanished with the collapse of National Socialism. Many intellectuals died in combat, others were tried and imprisoned, even executed for their participation in war crimes. The survivors were left totally orphaned. Disoriented or censored, they could not continue with their work during the postwar period and little by little they forgot the meaning of their efforts.

After the Reich's defeat, the "Allied Control Council" issued the order JCS 1067 mandating the requisition and destruction of all kinds of Nazi literature. All publications from 1933 to 1945 in all areas, including politics, philosophy, history, science, poetry, sports and even manuals, calendars, all textbooks, folklore publications, children's stories, invaluable scientific and cultural research, and more, were destroyed by pulping. The Allied Control Council confiscated, banned and destroyed all copies that could be found of more than 35,000 individual titles. The complete list published as "Allied Censorship in Postwar Germany" (*Alliierte Zensur im Nachkriegsdeutschland*) reports on the largest ideological censorship operation in history. The plan of the Allied occupation authorities was systematic and executed as far as possible, until the last copy of a particular title was destroyed.

Another chapter of this bibliographic censorship was the sending of requisitioned material to the Allied countries. The US Library of Congress confiscated nearly two million titles, patents, dissertations, theses, diaries, official letters and documents, including a part of Hitler's personal library, Himmler's private diaries, and countless other important official documents. Timothy Ryback, in his work on the remains of Hitler's personal library, mentions the neglected state of this invaluable resource on Nazi ideology. The Soviet Union, meanwhile, confiscated the best of German literature including almost all medieval manuscripts. It was impossible to know with any degree of certainty the scope of ideological and cultural booty retained by the other Allied nations until recently. Altogether, 8 million university documents, studies, books and other items were lost in the destruction of Reich universities and government buildings during Allied bombings, according to UNESCO's paper "Lost Memory" and books such as "After the Reich: The Brutal History of the Allied Occupation"

Twilight of Men

by Giles MacDonogh.

Thousands of works of art created during the Third Reich also fell into allied hands. Any material work that recalled Nazi ideology was requisitioned and taken out of the public eye. Peter Adam, a researcher on so-called "Third Reich art", tells us how difficult it is to understand this cultural production in the aftermath of the almost superstitious postwar Allied censorship.

> During the last months of the war National Socialism hid its art in antiaircraft shelters. When the Americans arrived in 1945 they discovered an immense amount of paintings, sculptures, tapestries and furniture. Almost all so-called official art was shipped to the United States where it was locked up by the Department of Defense. A committee of historians agreed that no work showing swastikas or any other Nazi symbol should be returned. However in 1950, 1,650 works are returned and in 1986 another 6,255. These returned works were hidden in warehouses. Some fear that they have evil powers that could revive National Socialist thinking»[221]

This tremendous and shocking operation of cultural and ideological destruction is the largest in history, so a complete panoramic study of the cultural and political revolution of National Socialism will never be possible.

But even regarding the historical sources that have been conserved one must be very careful. The meticulous British historian David Irving warns of the unpleasant historical work facing a researcher of the Nazi era:

> I have been startled by the number of such 'diaries' which close scrutiny proves to have been faked or tampered with – invariably to Hitler's disadvantage. Two different men claimed to possess the entire diaries of Vice Admiral Wilhelm Canaris....

---

221 Peter Adam. *Art of the Third Reich*

National Socialism - Its Principles and Philosophy

the Eva Braun diaries published by the film actor Luis Trenker were largely forged from the memoirs written decades earlier by Countess Irma Larisch-Wallersee.... The oft quoted diaries of Himmler's and Ribbentrop's Berlin masseur Felix Kersten are equally fictitious.... Similarly the 'diaries' published by Rudolf Semler are phoney too.... Ciano spent the months after his dismissal in February 1943 rewriting and 'improving' the diaries himself, which makes them readable but useless for the purposes of history. Ribbentrop warned about the forgery in his prison memoirs – he claimed to have seen Ciano's real diaries in September 1943.... Luftwaffe Chief of Staff Karl Koller's real shorthand diary often bears no resemblance to the version he published... The 'diaries' of the late General Gerhard Engel, who served as [Hitler's] army adjutant... whatever they are, they are not contemporaneous diaries.

The diaries of Himmler have largely vanished – partly carried off as trophies to Moscow... The diaries of Hans Lammers, Wilhelm Brückner, and Karl Bodenschatz vanished into American or French hands; those of Professor Theo Morell vanished, too.

Nicolaus von Below's are probably in Moscow. Alfred Rosenberg's remaining unpublished diaries were illicitly held by the late Dr. Robert M. W. Kempner, an American lawyer based in Frankfurt.... The rest of Milch's diaries... have vanished, as have General Alfred Jodl's diaries....Only a brief fragment of Benito Mussolini's diary survives: the SS copied the originals and returned them to him in January 1945, but both the originals and the copy placed in Ribbentrop's files are missing now. The important diaries of Rudolf Schmundt were, unhappily, burned.[222]

Irving's account goes on to detail the process of editorial falsification. When comparing the original manuscripts with the published

---

[222] David Irving. *Hitler's War*

memoirs of Hitler's assistant *SS-Hauptsturmführer* Karl Krause and of *SS-Brigadeführer* Walter Schellenberg, Himmler's chief of counter-intelligence, Irving noted important changes made by the publishing house.

In the immediate postwar period the scientific diffusion of the *Life-Laws* also suffered important censorship that removed them from the cultural sphere. UNESCO issued the "Declarations on Race" that refuted the National Socialist Worldview and the scientific world entered a phase where ideologies which detract from the natural laws of man became the basis for much scientific and political philosophy. Today, biological science has partially reversed this trend. Evolutionism and modern molecular biology have taken up a view that takes the relentless laws of nature into account in human dynamics. However, this scientific knowledge has had no expression in politics or culture. On the contrary, the cultural-political canon of postmodernism is highly abstract. Postmodern western man and society are based on values that are not supported by an order of ecological balance. It is probable that never before have abstract ideologies had as much cultural power and influence as they do today. The divorce between culture and natural laws is as a great challenge in establishing the foundations for successful communities to evolve and develop. This problem, warned of by Nietzsche more than 150 years ago, will apparently remain momentarily unanswered:

> Morality asks: How should one act? That question, in the mouth of a species that has acted for millennia, is really absurd.

The truth is that evolution never stops, and the question —already being asked by modern biologists— is what would be the biological consequences of evolution without either natural selection or public policies tending toward evolutionary improvement. The postmodern response seems to be a path that bets on turning aside from Nature, appeasing the counter-selective consequences by means of palliative medicines, surgical interventions or biogenetic manipulation, a fundamental industry for a culture devoid of the selective barrier.

The social, economic and even racial policies of National Socialism were the products of their historical moment. The essence of Nazism cannot be understood from policy, since this was merely a constantly changing means to an end. To focus on policies to define Nazism is to assess an ideology vis-à-vis partial and secondary concepts.

The Nazis intuited the new and profound challenges that they should face in a postwar period and for that they developed new policies and horizons that would surely alter many of their prior accomplishments, even the most characteristic ones. During the 12 years of government, National Socialism created successful policies as well as others that were unsuccessful, policies that promoted the common good and others that produced pain and suffering, brilliant policies along with brutal ones. However, beyond this game of trial-and-error, the goal was always the same: to create a society that fully assimilated the *Life-Laws* in order to ensure the health, preservation and biological improvement of the community. National Socialism was a political plan of improvement and social progress through increasing the biological value of the population. This is the entire scope of the NS Worldview and its *Life-Laws*. This was it's ideological compass and the only real objectives of the National Socialist revolution.

Bibliography

The largest collection of National Socialist ideological texts in the original language is available on Internet Archive (www.archive.org), a foundation dedicated to "universal access to knowledge" with 400 billion titles available online. In the English language, Third Reich Books (www.third-reich-books.com) has many and varied offerings.

Adam, Peter. *Art of the Third Reich.*

Anderton, Rex. *A study of various Nationalist appropriations of Nietzsche in the Weimar Republic.*

Allied censorship in postwar Germany. *List of prohibited books.*

Army Personnel Office. *Why Do We Fight?*

Avdeyev, Vladimir. *Raciology: the Science of the Hereditary Traits of Peoples.*

Backhaus, Jürgen; Drechsler, Wolfgang: *Friedrich Nietzsche Economy and Society.*

Bäumler, Alfred. *Hellas and Germania.*

Bäumler, Alfred. *Nietzsche and National Socialism.*

Bäumler, Alfred. *Nietzsche, philosopher and politician.*

Barber, Sandro. *Alfred Bäumler and the cult of the hero.*

Beck, Hermann. *The fateful alliance, German conservatives and Nazis in 1933.*

Borman, Martin. *National Socialism and Christianity are irreconcilable.*

Bouhler, Philipp. *Adolf Hitler: A Short Sketch of His Life.*

Bullock, Alan. *Hitler, a study of tyranny.*

Brito, José de. *The thought of Ernst Krieck.*

Brücher, Heinz. *Inheritance and breeding.*

Carrio, Ursula. *Nietzsche and agonal philosophy.*

Cocks, Geoffrey. *Psychotherapy in the Third Reich.*

Combs, William L. *The Voice of the SS: A History of the SS Journal 'Das Schwarze Korps'.*

D'Alquen, Gunther. *Form and content.*

D'Alquen, Gunther. *The power of the heart.*

D'Alquen, Gunther. *The spiritual crisis.*

D'Alquen, Gunther. *Compendium of articles from the newspaper "Das Schwarzen Korps".*

Darré, Walther. Race. *A New Nobility Based on Blood And Soil.*

Darré, Walther. Race. *National Socialist Racial Policy.*

Deichmann, Ute. *Biologists Under Hitler.*

Degrelle, Leon. *Hitler for a thousand years.*

Dietrich, Otto. *The philosophical foundations of National Socialism.*

Dingler, Hugo. *Method instead of Epistemology and Philosophy of Science.*

Domarus, Max. *Hitler speeches and proclamations.*

Eckstein, Ludwig. *The biological meaning of selection.*

Edler, Frank H. W. *Alfred Bäumler about Hölderlin and the Greeks.*

Eggers, Kurt. *Father of all things.*

Eggers, Kurt. *Hostility.*

Eggers, Kurt. *The freedom of the warrior.*

Ellersieck, Kurt. *Our life.*

Flood, Charles Bracelen. *Hitler, the road to power.*

Frercks, Rudolf. *German demographic policy.*

Frercks, Rudolf. *The racial awakening of the German people.*

Gauger Kurt. *Political Medicine.*

Gasman, Daniel. *The Scientific Origins of National Socialism.*

Gehlen, Arnold. *The State and philosophy.*

Geuter, Ulfried. *The professionalization of Psychology in Nazi Germany.*

Goebbles, Joseph. *Diaries 1942-1943. Edited by Louis Lochner*

Gohdes, Otto. Educational Paper (Schulungsbrief).

Bibliography

Günther, Hans F.K. *The Religious Attitudes of the Indo-Europeans.*

Günther, Hans F.K. *Nobility and race.*

Günther, Hans F.K. *People, State, Inheritance and Selection.*

Gross, Walther. *Nazi racial thought.*

Gross, Walther. *The Racial thinking in the world.*

Gross, Walther. *Worldview and racial hygiene.*

Griessdorf, Harry. *Struggle As Life-Law.*

Griessdorf, Harry. *Our Worldview.*

Haeckel, Ernst. *The Riddle of the universe.*

Hatheway, Jay. *In perfect formation. SS Ideology and the SS-Junkerschule Tolz.*

Hartl, Albert (Anton Holzner). *Master Life.*

Hartl, Albert (Anton Holzner). *God's Law.*

Hartl, Albert (Anton Holzner). *Eternal Front.*

Hartl, Albert (Anton Holzner). *Priest Power.*

Härtle, Heinrich. *Nietzsche and National Socialism.*

Heidegger, Martin. *The end of metaphysics.*

Heidegger, Martin. *The fundamental question of philosophy.*

Heidegger, Martin. *Nietzsche Vol I. The Will to power as Art.*

Heidegger, Martin. *Nietzsche Vol. II. The Eternal Return.*

Heidegger, Martin. *Nietzsche: Vol. III. The Will to power as knowledge and Metaphysics.*

Heidegger, Martin. *Nietzsche Vol. IV. Nihilism.*

Heidegger, Martin. *Heraclitus Seminar.*

Heidegger, Martin. *On the essence of truth.*

Himmler, Heinrich. *Speech to the Wehrmacht officer corps.*

Hitler, Adolf. *Table Talk.*

Hitler, Adolf. *Speeches and Proclamations 1932-1945.* Edited by Max Domarus.

Hitler, Adolf. *Discourses 1933-1938.* Edited by Editorial Kamerad.

National Socialism - Its Principles and Philosophy

Hitler, Adolf. *Mein Kampf.*

Hitler, Adolf. *Second Book.*

Heeck, Ingo. *Spheres of influence and Völkisch legal thought. Reinhard Höhn's notion of Europe.*

Hutton, Christopher M. *Race and the Third Reich.*

Heydrich, Reinhard. *Transformations of our struggle.*

Ingrao, Christian. *Believe and destroy. Intellectuals in the SS War Machine.*

Irving, David. *Hitler's War.*

Ivanov, Avdeev. *The Creator of Racial Pedagogy Ernst Krieck.*

Jaensch, E.R. [Erich]. *Eidetic Imagery, And Typological Methods of Investigation.*

Joerges, Christian. *Europe a Grossraum?*

Joerges, Christian. *Darker legacies of Law in Europe.*

Junker, Thomas. *The Architects of The Evolutionary Synthesis in National Socialist Germany.*

Kerhl, Hans. *Crisis Manager in the Third Reich.*

Klöcket, Hans. *Artist and soldier.*

Krannhals, Paul. *The organic Worldview*

Krieck, Ernst. *Volkisch—Political Anthropology.*

Krieck, Ernst. Sketch of the Science of Education.

Krieck, Ernst. *The German of the German Language Society.*

Krieck, Ernst. *Philosophy.*

Krieck, Ernst. *Philosophy of Education.*

Krieck, Ernst. *The Racial-Völkisch-Political Conception of History.*

Krieck, Ernst. Renewal of the German University.

Lebovic, Nitzan. The beauty and terror of Lebensphilosophie. Ludwig Klages, Walter Benjamin, and Alfred Bäumler.

Lechler, Jörg. *The Swastika, History of a Symbol.*

Leers, Johann Von. Odal. The laws of the life of an eternal Germany.

Lorenz, Konrad. About aggressiveness.

Bibliography

Mayerhofer, J. The Order of the Clans.

Magdalinski, Tara. Beyond Hitler. Alfred Bäumler, ideology and physical education in the Third Reich.

Maser, Werner. Notes and letters of Hitler.

Mess, Bernard. *The Science of the Swastika.*

Mosse, George. *Nazi Culture: Intellectual, Sultural and Social Life in the Third Reich.*

Mullin, John. *The impact of National Socialist policies on urban planning in prewar Germany.*

Nathan, Otto. *Nazi War Finance and Banking.*

National Potitische Aufklärungschriften. Vol I. Fundamentals of the National Socialist Worldview.

National Potitische Aufklärungschriften. Vol II. The Origin of Our People.

Neumann, Franz. Behemoth. Behemoth, The Structure and Practice of National Socialism.

Nietzsche, Friedrich. Complete Works.

NS Leadership Staff of the High Command of the Armed Forces. *Struggle as Life Law*

Oesterle, Friedrich. Everything has its order.

Pabel, Horst. Roman Church and Raciology.

Pacyna, Günther. Basic Law of the Peasantry.

Rabinbach, Anson. The Third Reich Sourcebook.

Reich, Fritz. Birth and End of the World in Aryan Myth.

Reichsschulungsamt der NSDAP. Educational Sheets (Schulungsbriefe) editor Otto Gohdes.

Reichorganizationleiter der NSDAP. The Educational Sheets (Der Schulungsbrief).

Reichorganizationleiter der NSDAP. NSDAP organization book.

Reinhold, Arthur; Ritsch, Hermann Arthur. The economy in the National Socialist Worldview.

Reinert, Erik: A human question too human. Nietzsche, Die Soziale Frage, and the German School of Economic History.

Reinert, Erik: Creative Destruction in the Economy: Nietzsche, Sombart, Schumpeter.

Reinsperger, Regina. Otto Ohlendorf.

Riis-Knudsen, Povl H.: National Socialism, the Biological Worldview.

Rieppel, Olivier. Hugo Dingler and the philosophical foundations of the evolutionary synthesis in Germany.

Rosenberg, Alfred. The myth of the twentieth century. An assessment of the soul-spiritual struggles of the forms in our time.

Rosenberg, Alfred. The struggle for our worldview.

Rosenberg, Alfred. Philosophical foundations of National Socialism.

Rosenberg, Alfred. Thesis on the Worldview.

Rosenberg, Alfred. Gestalt und Leben, speech 1938.

Schaefer, Heinz Oskar. *General aspects of the National Socialist Worldview*, in *Educational Writings for National Politics. Vol. I*

Schaper, Ernst. German-German authority.

Schultz, Wolfgang. The Zarathustra of Nietzsche and the historical.

Schultz, Wolfgang. Basic ideas of National Socialist Cultural Policy.

Schwarz, Martin A. Bäumler and His Disciples.

Schrempf, Claus. Nietzsche the prophet.

Schilling, Heinar. Reflections on the Worldview. Compendium of articles from the newspaper "Das Schwarzen Korps".

Schinke, Gerhart. The eternal *Life-Laws*.

Schinke, Gerhart. What do the Peoples die of? I.

Schinke, Gerhart. What do the Peoples die of? II.

Schmidt, Julius. Military science,

Sedgwick, Peter. Nietzschean economy.

Simon, Gerd. The Rosenberg School of Higher Education.

Simon, Gerd. Scientific policy of the SS Security Service.

Simon, Gerd. Type, selection and extermination. The unknown dictionary project of the SS Main Office.

Six, Franz Alfred (Under the pseudonym Schwarz, Dieter). Attack against the

Bibliography

National Socialist Worldview.

Six, Franz Alfred (Under the pseudonym Schwarz, Dieter). The great lie of political Catholicism.

Six, Franz Alfred. The power of the written word.

Six, Franz Alfred (Under the pseudonym Schwarz, Dieter). International Judaism. Organization, power and policies.

Six, Franz Alfred. The mass and street propaganda.

Six, Franz Alfred (Under the pseudonym Schwarz, Dieter). Masonry. Ideology, organization and politics.

Speer, Albert. *Infiltration: How Heinrich Himmler Schemed to Build an SS Industrial Empire.*

Spehr, Harold. Were the Ancient Germans "Ecstatics"?

SS-Hauptamt. *The SS is calling you.*

SS-Hauptamt. *Bolshevism Jewish sub-humanity.*

SS-Hauptamt. *SS Mate Selection and Race.*

SS-Hauptamt. *Believe and fight.*

SS-Hauptamt. *Guidance books (Leitheft).*

SS-Hauptamt. *The NSDAP path.*

SS-Hauptamt. *The subhuman.*

SS-Hauptamt. *Guide for the Celebration of the Führer's Birthday.*

SS-Hauptamt. *Black Squads. (Das Schwarze Korps).*

SS-Hauptamt. *Notebooks for the teaching of the Worldview. 5 volumes, 25 themes.*

SS-Hauptamt. *Teaching Plan for Worldview Education of the SS and Police.*

SS-Hauptamt. *Racial Policy.*

SS-Hauptamt. *Europe Defense.*

SS-Hauptamt. Magazine for the Houses of the Troop SS.

SS-Hauptamt. *Schutzstaffel as an anti-Bolshevik organization.*

SS-Hauptamt. *Seven hundred books for the National Socialist Library.*

SS-Hauptamt. *SS-Man and Blood Questions.*

SS-Hauptamt. *Victory of arms, victory of child.*

Stackelberg, Roderick. The Nazi Germany Sourcebook: An Anthology of Texts.

Stolfi, R. H. S. Hitler: Beyond Evil and Tyranny.

Staudenmaier, Peter. *Between Occultism and Fascism.*

Tooze, Adam. *The Wages of Destruction.*

Tratz, Eduard Paul. Struggle in nature.

Thibaut, Edwige. The Order SS. Ethics and ideology of the Black Order.

Usadel, Georg. Discipline and order. Foundations of National Socialist Ethics.

Varshizky, Amit. Mind and soul in the National Socialist Weltanschauung.

Weikart, Richard. *Hitler's Ethics: The Nazi Pursuit of Evolutionary Progress.*

Weikart, Richard. *The Role of Darwinism in Nazi Racial Thought.*

Weiss, Sheila Faith. *The Nazi Symbiosis: Human Genetics and Politics in the Third Reich.*

Weitzel, Fritz. Celebrations of the SS family.

Weitzel, Fritz. Explanations to the law of the Order SS.

Weitzel, Fritz. Law of Order SS.

Woodward, Ashley. Understanding Nietzscheanism.

Ziegler, Matthes. Faith warrior, honor warrior. Germanic Breviary for Hitler's warriors.